So, About That... A Year Of
and Pop Culture

Seren Sensei

Forward

Wow. I can't believe this is finally finished. The past year has been a roller coaster, starting from the day all of our lives changed, August 9, 2014. From the moment Mike Brown fell, a movement began to grow, seeds of discontent that eventually grew into a flame fanning across the country. I found myself angry and hurt, prone to emotional outbursts that were only worsened by sleepless nights spent watching live streams of the goings on in Ferguson. I was unable to turn away, but I soon discovered I needed an outlet for my thoughts. My husband suggested I upload and record my rants to YouTube, and my channel, Sensei Aishitemasu, was born (and for everyone wondering- the name was chosen by my participation in the 'Pacific Rim' fandom on tumblr. They were the last words spoken to my favorite character, Stacker Pentecost, who was played by Idris Elba).

For the first few months I posted in relative obscurity. But, slowly, something interesting began to happen- the channel started to grow. A little community formed, people sharing stories and having discussions in the comment section. I couldn't help but notice the safe space that began to thrive, Black folks especially interacting with one another, finding solace- and sometimes, venting their rage and fear, without being judged or told to be silent. The place I had created for myself had turned into an outlet for others, as well, and over time, it developed a kind of consciousness of it's own. I went from speaking strictly on Ferguson to other issues of injustice and police brutality, gradually expanding the channel to cover all race-related topics and pop culture.

My regulars stuck with me through it all, and soon, our ranks swelled to over 11,000 subscribers at the time of publishing of this book. Many of you joked that you took notes while watching my videos (which can skew long- sorry!) and some requested supplementary materials to read along. I have always included fairly detailed information in the description boxes for my videos, so I started there, expanding on theories and concepts. Some of the material in this book will be familiar, but a lot of it is new- I mined through the past year's worth of videos for inspiration, carefully preparing these short essays on contemporary race relations and pop culture.

This book is for everyone that has been with me since the beginning, as well as everyone new; it's for my husband, without whom the channel probably wouldn't exist (great suggestion, babe!); it's for everyone tired of tip-toeing around race, everyone that has been told they are 'pulling the race card' or 'making everything about race;' it's for the cities of Ferguson, Charleston, Baltimore- and last, but certainly not least, it's for Mike Brown. Vonderrit Myers. Aiyana Stanley-Jones. Sandra Bland. And all of our brothers and sisters lost in the struggle.

This book is for YOU. Thank you.

Yes, All white People Are Racist

Stay with me.

When you say 'all white people' they rush to claim that is unfair because they are 'individuals;' but this sense of individualism in and of itself is a privilege. Individualism is a facet of privilege.

Folks get MADT when you say #AllWhitePeople, even Black folks, because we've been trained to look at white people as 'individuals' even though they are conditioned to look at us as a group. White people are raised to believe they are unique, special snowflakes- individuals capable of achieving whatever they set their minds to- while Black people are raised to believe we are part of a monolithic group; one that at any minute can be seen as a threat so we must act accordingly so as to make everyone around us *comfortable. *

We do not have the privilege of individualism. So spare me your whining about *not all White people. *

Yes, all white people.

All white people are products of a racist, white supremacist system, and therefore are indoctrinated with racist, white supremacist teachings. Can racism be unlearned? I think, yes. But most white people DON'T unlearn it, because they can't even admit they have a problem.

You can't opt out of the system. You can't opt out of your privilege. You can't opt out of its benefits if you're born with white skin.

And it's funny how we understand this when we're talking about other forms of pathology. We understand that people growing up in abusive households have higher chances of being impacted by abuse. We understand that soldiers coming back from violent war zones have higher chances of being affected by post-traumatic stress disorder. We understand that people in certain environments will be psychologically impacted in certain ways.

But start talking about learned racism and, all of a sudden, everything we know about the human brain goes out the window because every white person is a unique special snowflake (with the magical mutant x abilities to not be influenced by their surroundings and the constant barrage of racist, white supremacist propaganda).

Dear white people: You are not omega level mutants able to control things with your mind. You are not Jean Gray. You have been born into this racist, sexist, capitalist, white supremacist society and from birth you have been imbued with its beliefs.

(And white people love bringing up their parents and their families and how every white parent had a perfect non-racist upbringing. Yeah, okay. Even if I believed that, which I don't, you still watch television and movies, you still read books, you still go to school, you still have to participate in society outside of the home and white supremacist ideology is EVERYWHERE.)

The most you can do is understand your privilege, use it to spread awareness, and WORK to unlearn your destructive, parasitic behavior. That's how you white ally. And if you are not working to unlearn racism don't speak to me. If you're feeling so bold go address your fellow racist whites, not me. Why are you comfortable telling me #NotAllWhites but you're not comfortable telling your fellow white people #NotAllBlacks? Because deep down, even if it's just on a subconscious level, you have a superiority complex. You think you are better than me and you have a right to come in my black space and try to 'correct' me. This is a racist microaggression and it's a form of white supremacy.

The ONLY thing you should be saying to be is that you recognize that you were born into a racist, white supremacist system that imbued you with racist ideals from birth. That you recognize your racism, privilege, and inherent bias and are actively working to unlearn it. If you are not saying that then you are not saying anything, and you don't have permission to speak to me.

YOU DONT HAVE PERMISSION TO TALK TO ME.
#YESALLWHITEPEOPLE

On Integration

I think integration was a trap.

I think it was a mistake.

And I think the ideals of integration were extremely flawed.

The entire principles of segregation revolved around separate but equal; and instead of fighting to be equal, integrationists fought against being separate. I think this was a mistake. Because once people become equals, integration happens naturally. White people STILL don't see us as equals, even though aware no longer separate, which is why we even have to say 'black lives matter.' We were forced together without dealing with the issues of not being seen as equal to whites.

And that means that we were never actually integrated. We were merely desegregated, assimilated, and colonized. There is a difference between integrated and desegregated. I have some definitions:

Racial integration, or simply integration, includes desegregation (the process of ending systematic racial segregation). In addition to desegregation, integration includes goals such as leveling barriers to association, creating equal opportunity regardless of race, and the development of a culture that draws on diverse traditions, rather than merely bringing a racial minority into the majority culture. Desegregation is largely a legal matter, integration largely a social one.

Cultural assimilation is the process by which a person or a group's language and/or culture come to resemble those of another group. The term is used to refer to both individuals and groups, and in the latter case it can refer to either immigrant diasporas or native residents that come to be culturally dominated by another society. Assimilation may involve either a quick or gradual change depending on circumstances of the group.

Colonization (or colonization) occurs whenever there is a large-scale migration of any one or more groups of people to a colonial area. The migrants, who can also be called colonizers, keep "strong links" with their previous country, and thus obtain tremendous "privileges" over other people living in the area being colonized.

So I think we can all agree that racial integration never actually happened. Civil rights era activists did not take care of business. Do I respect what they did? Yes, absolutely. It took a lot of courage, hindsight is always 20/20, AND I believe that the untimely death of MLK stalled the movement. But it is undeniable that their actions led to where we are today.

Because the core principles of integration were flawed. We fought against being separate instead of fighting to be equal. We placed more value on being next to white people than on our own equality. And that is a crucial distinction. Because there is an inherent implication there that white people are superior to us and therefore we will be superior if we can be next to them, if we can have what they have, instead of building up our own. And towards the end of MLKs life he was talking about economic self-reliance within the Black community and a lot of people actually speculate that that is what really got him killed. The work was never finished. The movement stalled, like I said, somewhere in the middle, after his death and the death of Malcolm X.

And Malcolm X actually gave a very popular speech, "You Don't Integrate With a Sinking Ship;" where he stresses the importance of unity and self-reliance in the Black community.

Malcolm's approach was the only way we'd see Dr. King's dream. He was the one talking about Black Nationalism, control of black economics, building up the community, etc. Black people truly becoming equals at the table is better than forced integration with people that have learned to hate you for several generations and control all the institutions you depend on for further stability and development.

And that's it, right? And that's the thing. I completely agree. I feel like the civil rights activists did things backwards. They focused on removing the separation first and THEN there were plans to focus on destabilizing hate, on creating economic and financial equality, and equality in terms of infrastructure, etc. I think that the fight for equality and the destabilization of white supremacist beliefs should have come first. Make the Black community equal to the white community in terms of businesses we own, products we create, jobs we create, infrastructure, political clout, you know, focus on building up our community and integration will happen naturally. The separation will dissipate because it will HAVE to. Because you can't ignore a superpower. You can't ignore an economic powerhouse. You can't say, 'Well these niggers are inferior' when they are self-sustaining and creating and financially secure and so on and so forth. You can't.

"Are you advocating for segregation? Because we tried it that way and it didn't work."

I know that's what you're thinking. But... did it not work? Really? Let's look at it from a logical standpoint and not an emotional one. Because I know even the word, 'segregation,' creates an emotional response in people. But think about it. During segregation and pre-integration, ECONOMICALLY Black people thrived more than now. When white people weren't burning down our communities, our communities thrived more than now. Our nuclear families thrived more than now. Pre-integration, Black women had higher marriage rates than white women. There were fewer Black men in the prison system than now. All of these things that we see destroying the Black community, from the school to prison pipeline, to the war on drugs, to the stop and frisk aka broken windows policy, all these things, all manner of institutionalized laws and action, were reactions from white supremacist power structures to forced 'integration.' They had to find other ways to keep us oppressed. If we had left them alone and they had left us alone, who knows where we would be today?

You had thousands of Black owned businesses that were thriving during this time of pre-forced integration.

You had Johnson Products Company, which was started in 1954 and was the first Black-owned company to be listed on the American Stock Exchange. (One of their most popular products is Afro Sheen.)

You had the Madame C.J. Walker Manufacturing Company, founded in 1910, which led to Madame CJ Walker becoming the first self-made female millionaire in American history.

You had the American Negro Theater, founded in 1940, which created stage production as well as Black radio programming, and had an aggressive acting training program, which trained great actors such as Sidney Poitier, Harry

Belafonte, Ruby Dee, Ossie Davis. Great Black actors being trained and taught by other Black actors.

We were business owners. We ran our own institutions, from school systems to sports leagues to transportation companies. The unemployment rate for black teens in 1965 was 29%; today it's 40%. There were Black communities that thrived while their white neighbors were poor, like Tulsa, Oklahoma. And we gave that all away to be fake integrated aka assimilated into white society. So now our best and brightest have to be taught by white people. We agreed to be mentally colonized. Let's look at the definition of colonization again:

Colonization occurs whenever there is a large-scale migration of any one or more groups of people to a colonial area. The migrants, who can also be called colonizers, keep "strong links" with their previous country, and thus obtain tremendous "privileges" over other people living in the area being colonized.

Our minds were migrated into whiteness and white institutions, while white people kept their strong links and remained in positions of power with tremendous privilege over us within their institutions. And we agreed! We fought for that!

Economically, financially, and in terms of institutions, systems, being separated from whites worked for Black people. It is undeniable; you can't say it didn't work. What DIDN'T work for Black people was not economics. It was the idea of white supremacy. What didn't work for Black people was the constant fear of living under the domestic terrorism of public lynching's/hangings/beatings/rapes/attacks. What didn't work for Black people was institutionalized terror at the hands of civilians and police, wondering if today was the day you were going to be killed by a police officer or a vigilante with a gun. What didn't work for Black people was being called racial slurs and being treated like second-class citizens in the country of their birth. What didn't work for Black people was state-sanctioned violence. What didn't work for Black people were subpar school and work facilities and bathrooms and water fountains because they were in *Black* neighborhoods or because they were for Black people.

And in 2015, those things STILL don't work for Black people. Because they were NEVER addressed during forced 'integration.' In 2015, every last one of those things I just named STILL DOES NOT WORK FOR BLACK PEOPLE. Because we were never truly integrated. We were merely de-segregated, assimilated, and colonized. We gave up everything that we had built independent of white people post-Civil War for the LIE of integration. We were sold a dream. And that dream has become a nightmare.

And the only way to get back on track, in my humble opinion, is Black unification and Black independence.

There is a great Key and Peele skit about a place called 'Negrotown,' an all-Black town where Black people can go to be safe and free. THIS IS A SKIT IN 2015. And people still have the nerve to say, 'We tried segregation, it didn't work.' Well, what does this say about 'integration?' About our assimilation into white society? IT'S NOT WORKING.

So at a certain point you have to ask yourself, well why does Negrotown have to be a skit?

People love to say, again, 'You're advocating for segregation and that's WRONG!' Because we have this knee jerk reaction to whites and blacks being separated. But people are separated by culture all over the country. There are cultural enclaves scattered throughout the United States, especially in major metropolitan cities. Be they religious (Amish, Hasidic Jewish, Mormon) or ethnic/racial (Chinatown, Little Italy, Wash Heights) in nature. People love the idea of, "Going to Little Italy for some Italian food;" or "Going to Chinatown for some herbs," but they will screw their faces up and scream, 'That's racist!' at the thought of Black people wanting to live in Black neighborhoods, send their kids to Black schools, and patronize Black owned businesses.

No one bats an eyelash at Native American reservations, like the Seminole res in South Florida, which has it's OWN school system. There is no issue with Chinatown, a space where people of all the same race live and work together, supporting their own establishments like shops, restaurants, and banks. There is a huge Chinese bank on Canal St in NYC where all of the writing is in Chinese, all of the tellers are Chinese, if you are not Chinese or at the very least SPEAK Chinese, you are not going to be able to utilize that bank. But that is not seen as racist or problematic. Why? There is no issue with Little Russia in Coney Island.

People will support these enclaves all day and all night, yet talk of supporting BOBs or communities draws raised eyebrows and cries of racism. Start talking about Black enclaves and Black communities and watch people call you a segregationist. Why?

There is a very specific and very intense pushback against American Black people creating our own communities, systems, and businesses in this country... because white people have a very specific set of feelings of superiority, domination and ownership over black people to this day, mingled with fear of what will happen if we work together. Even if only on a subconscious level. It is there.

They are still indoctrinated with white supremacist beliefs from the time they are born that they are superior and that they are our masters. That they did everything, we did nothing, and we need them. #YesAllWhitePeople. White savior complex. It's taught in the school system. It's taught in the home. It's taught in the media. Black unification and Independence from them is terrifying to them and it's also terrifying to us. Because Black people have also been indoctrinated with these same beliefs; that white people are superior and that we need them to get things done like they are our parents.

You don't know how many comments I get saying, 'well, we NEED white allies.' Why? If white allies are there, cool whatever, but why do we NEED them? It's internalized white supremacy. And this mindset goes back to integration, where instead of fighting to be equal, we fought to not be separate. We fought to be next to precious white people. We fought to be right up under precious white people.

Black people and white people have a unique history in this country, unlike white people and really any other minority group here (which is also why it's infuriating when white people like to compare the disenfranchisement of Black people to other minority groups and say, 'Well, [insert POC group here] did it, why can't you?').

There is still an idea that Black Americans do not have a culture, and a prevailing sentiment that our lives and self-worth are inextricably enmeshed with white people. White people love the idea of certain types of people living together to preserve and embrace their cultures. There are whole shows about it, like

Growing up Amish, about My Big Fat Gypsy Wedding (even though Gypsy is a slur). They actually love the idea of separation because they love the idea of being able to enter into these cultural enclaves at will. But they do NOT like the idea of Black people doing the same. There is an inherent fear, an unconscious, subconscious bias towards large groups of Black people working together, a fear of what we will do, and this fear manifests itself in aggressive ways, be it the burning of Black Wall Street in Tulsa, OK, or the vehement claim that Black people supporting one another is somehow 'racist.' And this fear has been taught to us as well. There is a fear of supporting Black owned businesses. A fear of living in all Black neighborhoods. A fear of going to Historically Black Colleges and Universities (HBCUs). A fear that none of those things will be quality or good enough.

The lie of white supremacy has taught us that they are better than us, so for us to be 'equal,' we cannot be separate. We have to be able to attend THEIR schools, work at THEIR jobs, and shop in THEIR stores. We were taught by integration that our own was inferior, so to be 'equal,' we had to have exactly what white people had. We equate whiteness with privilege and luxury. We are Black white supremacists.

Our integration into white society (aka assimilation) was ultimately destructive to our community. Because instead of placing value on creating our own structures and institutions that were equal in QUALITY to what white people had, we became obsessed with proving we were worthy of THEIR structures. We became obsessed with receiving validation from white people, be it being able to go to that private, all-white school, work that white-owned corporate job, or buy from that white-owned European luxury brand. As I've said in other videos, we got into this mindset of, for something to be good, it had to be white. We abandoned our own businesses and communities for the trill of being able to shop, work, and live amongst white people- who we inherently think are better than us. And, again, while our schools and businesses withered and died, theirs flourished, with DOUBLE the resources coming in (their white money that they already had AND our black money). We literally paid our colonizers to further colonize us.

This widespread notion of non-Black as high-class, luxury, and superior is a direct result of integration. Black elitism, whether in academic or elsewhere, is the culmination of how years of unsound thinking in the black agenda against white supremacy has led to unsound strategy. It shows our intent to break free of it has been diluted by our foolish desire to be accepted by it or to prove it wrong by prospering within it, and it won't work. They'll never care; it's that simple- our strategy should begin there. Appealing to the white psyche by highlighting moral standards, which is really all we are doing at the end of the day with the books and social experiments etc., we are only saying "racism is wrong you should cut it out," needs to stop because they have in large already chosen their privilege over righteous action. It will take nothing short of a spiritual revolution for whites to step down from their sense of superiority in the name of humanity.

Isn't going to happen.

The social experiment of integration was a failure because the real issues- the pathology of racism white supremacy, the urge to own and dominate us, the feelings of superiority over us, the fear of groups of Black people together- none of that was ever dealt with.

Toni Morrison told y'all in 1975. [1]

I'm telling y'all in 2015.

Racism and the system of racism white supremacy is the problem. And it is white people's problem. And they're the ones that have to undo it. Stop trying to fix white people. Stop trying to prove yourselves to them. Stop trying to live around them, go to their schools, shop in their establishments, and stop trying to validate yourself by your proximity to whiteness. It is a burden and you don't have to do it anymore. (As Toni Morrison said. In 1975.)

What we should be focusing on is building a strong Black community. That is true equality. We can't keep wasting energy begging and begging and begging white people to validate our humanity. They're not going to do it because they're racist, which will stop them from listening to anything you have to say anyway because you're Black. And all of this begging comes from this

---

[1] Portland State, "Black Studies Center public dialogue. Pt. 2" May 30, 1975. Web. < https://soundcloud.com/portland-state-library/portland-state-black-studies-1/>.

integrationist mindset where white people still have ownership over us. Where you have to ask master for his permission.

I think marches and protests are important to show a united front to our enemies, to raise awareness about what's going on, and to build solidarity amongst Black people, but literally begging white people to recognize that we are human beings inherently places them in a position of power over us. Begging to be integrated into their schools and their stores and their lunch counters and their neighborhoods inherently put them into positions of power over us. Staging Bloody Sunday in Selma, Alabama to reach into the hearts and minds and television sets of white Americans so they could put pressure on President Lyndon B. Johnson to pass the Voting Rights Act, inherently put them into positions of power over us. And they still feel that power. They still feel that domination. They still feel that ownership.

White people DON'T own me and I'm not going to beg them for anything. I'm going to build what I can with my people, and I would advise you to do the same.

Reading List

1. Portland State, "Black Studies Center public dialogue. Pt. 2" May 30, 1975. Web. < https://soundcloud.com/portland-state-library/portland-state-black-studies-1/>.

2. "Five Ways Integration Underdeveloped Black America." *Atlanta Black Star*. December 9, 2013. Web. <http://atlantablackstar.com/2013/12/09/5-ways-integration-underdeveloped-black-america/>.

3. Llopis-Jepsen, Celia. "Pre-Brown, some black teachers lost jobs as integration approached." *The Topeka-Capital Journal*. May 16, 2014. Web. <http://cjonline.com/news/2014-05-16/1953-some-black-teachers-were-told-jobs-would-be-lost-if-integration-approved/>.

4. Blakeney, Barney. "How integration led to the decline of black-owned businesses." *Charleston City Paper*. March 12, 2009. Web. <http://www.charlestoncitypaper.com/charleston/how-integration-led-to-the-decline-of-black-owned-businesses/Content?oid=1113614/>.

5. Apollon, Dom; Zipper, Erin. "The Equity Gap, 1965-2013 [Infographic]." Colorlines. June 24, 2013. Web. < http://www.colorlines.com/content/equity-gap-1965-2013-infographic/>.

6. Van Leeuwen, David. "Marcus Garvey and the Universal Negro Improvement Association." National Humanities Center, n.d. Web. <http://nationalhumanitiescenter.org/tserve/twenty/tkeyinfo/garvey.htm/>.

7. Lawson, Steven F. "Segregation." Department of History, Rutgers, the State University of New Jersey. National Humanities Center, n.d. Web.

http://nationalhumanitiescenter.org/tserve/freedom/1865-1917/essays/segregation.htm/>.

8. "The History of Black-Owned Hotels." National Association of Black Hotel Owners, Operators, & Developers, n.d. Web. <http://www.nabhood.net/home/index.php/about-us/history-of-black-owned-hotels/>.

9. "'Our company': Safe Bus, started in 1926, was source of pride in Winston-Salem's black community." *Winston-Salem Journal.* June 16, 2013. Web. <http://www.journalnow.com/news/local/article_5613c01 8-d6f3-11e2-8657-0019bb30f31a.html/>.

On Privilege

This essay is going to be about privilege. A lot of people (black people with white friends, white people, and non-Black POC) have been requesting that I make an essay about not only privilege, but also what should privileged people do now that they're 'woke.'

The short answer: use your privilege.

I've noticed that every time I talk about 'isms,' defensive people come out of the woodwork, and I've come to the conclusion that 'isms' make dominant groups uncomfortable. Racism makes white people uncomfortable. Feminism/womanism/sexism makes men uncomfortable. Colorism makes light skinned people uncomfortable... and so on and so forth.

These 'isms' are about systems of privilege, and the reason all these things make people uncomfortable is because it forces them to confront their privilege. No one wants to feel like they have privilege; everyone wants to feel like they worked hard for what they have and that they deserve it. Drawing light to marginalized groups like Black people, or women, or people with darker skin, also brings light to those that benefit from not being marginalized

But privilege is an unavoidable offset of our society. It's not your fault that you have privilege; you were simply born into a society that places value on certain qualities. The mistake people make is in developing a sense of guilt over the fact that they happen to have those qualities- they feel guilty for having privilege so they deny it.

That knee jerk defensiveness is an emotional response and not a logical one, and to that I say: Get over it. Systems of privilege are a reality of the world we live in, so if you're going to feel guilt, don't deny it, instead, use your privilege to change things.

Denial is not productive (and, honestly, neither is guilt). Accept that you have privilege and use it to enter spaces where others might not be allowed and raise awareness. Make people uncomfortable. Recognize that you benefit from systems that are in place and work to undo that. Use your privilege to raise awareness.

I'm just saying, if you happen to possess those qualities that equate to privilege, use them to raise awareness of injustices, because, guess what? Racists use their privilege. They use their privilege in every way imaginable to keep Black people oppressed. Silence is consent. And it kills.

Reading List

1. Woods, Baynard. "Only white people can save themselves from racism and white supremacism." *The Washington Post.* Web. June 19, 2015. <http://www.washingtonpost.com/posteverything/wp/2015/06/19/only-white-people-can-save-themselves-from-racism-and-white-supremacism/?postshare=6821434719349847/>.

2. Leary, Patrick. "I Finally "Get" White Privilege and I'm Sorry." *The Daily Kos.* Web. August 20, 2014. <https://www.dailykos.com/story/2014/08/21/1323332/-I-Finally-Get-White-Privilege-and-I-m-Sorry/>.

3. Sharpe, Malik Nashad. "White Fragility, Silence, and Supremacy: Why All White Hands Are Bloody." Black Girl Dangerous. Web. June 19, 2015. <http://www.blackgirldangerous.org/2015/06/white-fragility-silence-and-supremacy-why-all-of-your-hands-are-bloody/>.

4. Lemieux, Jamilah. "White Silence Kills 9 in Charleston." *Ebony.* Web. June 19, 2015. http://www.ebony.com/news-views/white-silence-kills-9-in-charleston-503#ixzz3djEMdWqx/>.

5. Murphy, Carla. "Peggy McIntosh Sets Record Straight on White Privilege." Colorlines. Web. May 14, 2014. http://www.colorlines.com/articles/peggy-mcintosh-sets-record-straight-white-privilege/>.

6. DiAngelo, Robin. "White Fragility: Why It's So Hard to Talk to White People About Racism." The Good Men Project. Web. April 9, 2015. <http://goodmenproject.com/featured-content/white-fragility-why-its-so-hard-to-talk-to-white-people-about-racism-twlm/#sthash.lndpbOjP.dpuf/>.

7. McIntosh, Peggy. "White Privilege: Unpacking the Invisible Knapsack." n.p. Web. n.d. http://www.deanza.edu/faculty/lewisjulie/White%20Privilege%20Unpacking%20the%20Invisible%20Knapsack.pdf/>.

PSA: You Don't Have To Let Microaggressions Go

Racial microaggressions are behaviors that are not overtly racist but still cause the damaging effects of racism; i.e. dehumanization, discrimination, etc. This unintended discrimination generally manifests itself in the form insulting and/or dismissive behavior, reinforcement of stereotypes, or brief, every day exchanges meant to demean, degrade, or cause discomfort to a minority group on behalf of the majority group.

Psychologist and Columbia University professor Derald Wing Sue defines microaggressions as "...send[ing] denigrating messages to certain individuals because of their group membership," and she describes microaggressions as generally happening below the awareness of well-intentioned members of the dominant culture. [2] Microaggressions are considered to be different from deliberate acts of racism (such as the use of slurs or epithets), because the people perpetrating microaggressions often intend no offense and are completely unaware they are causing harm.

---

[2] Paludi, Michele A. (2012). *Managing Diversity in Today's Workplace: Strategies for Employees and Employers.* Praeger.

Letting microaggressions go reinforces the behavior, and Black people are trained to let these things go, it was a part of our colonization.

Stop. Take up space. Make white people uncomfortable.

Challenge them when they say out of pocket things, especially people you don't know in public places. A lot of the time all it even takes is a direct question forcing them to recognize their ignorance and hatefulness, even if they are not intentionally being that way.

Side note: While microaggressions are often used when speaking about race, it is also possible to be the victim of microaggressions for many other 'isms'- like sexism or homophobia, with the use of flippant, disparaging remarks meant to *other* you and your behavior. You don't have to accept this, and the people making these remarks are not your friends.

Reading List:

1. Paludi, Michele A. (2012). *Managing Diversity in Today's Workplace: Strategies for Employees and Employers*. Praeger.

So, About Those Nicki Minaj #VMAs Tweets.... And The DashCam Footage of Sandra Bland

So, the 2015 MTV Video Music Awards nominees were recently announced, and after an awards season where both film and music were extremely whitewashed, MTV followed the trend with a list of nominations that was overwhelmingly white and headed by Taylor Swift (with multiple nominations for her cameo-heavy video for 'Bad Blood').

Rapper Nicki Minaj was not pleased, and late last night, she released a series of tweets about the VMA nominations, where she spoke on the lack of nominations for her record-breaking videos for hits 'Anaconda' and 'Feeling Myself.' She mentioned the fact that Black women are often the influencers of popular culture without any recognition, and also vented her feeling that if she were a 'different' (aka white) artist, her videos and music would be more recognized. She essentially blasted structural racism in the music industry.

VMA frontrunner Swift, feeling some type of perceived slight at Minaj's words, directly replied with a statement on how Nicki was being 'divisive' instead of happy for the women on the list (regardless of race), and also implied that perhaps 'one of the men' on the list took her spot. The two ended up in a war of words that, in addition to Minaj's tweets on structural racism, also highlighted the issues within white feminism, wherein white women often ask Black women to ignore race in favor of gender.

When Minaj airs her grievances with an industry that does not recognize her influence because of her race and Swift asks Minaj to just be happy so many women were nominated, even if they were all white, she is essentially telling Minaj to shut up and take one for the team. She is asking Nicki to ignore structural racism, which Swift only has the power to do because structural racism in the music industry doesn't affect her as a white person. Her accusations of 'divisiveness' are a prime example of the way white feminists flex their white privilege against women of color, and Black women in particular.

As if this weren't enough, this entire back-and-forth also occurred at the same time arrest footage of the recently deceased Sandra Bland was released. The dash-cam video reveals a violent confrontation between the young Black woman and her arresting officer, which resulted in her face-down on the ground, and many found their social media accounts split between Nicki's tweets and the arrest footage, arguing on which was more important.

This is silly and annoying because, in my opinion, both are important. We all care about what happened to Sandra. But what happened to Nicki was ALSO violence against black women, and that's the bigger picture. It is not about the award.

This is about systems that reward whiteness and overlook, erase, and punish Blackness. This is about violence against Black women, whether we are being arrested and killed, OR being overlooked and discriminated against in artistic endeavors or our workplaces- like Nicki Minaj. It's about the consistent lack of recognition of Black women's contributions to culture. And it's about narratives that are pushed when Black women even dare to stand up for ourselves.

The media jumped in on both the Sandra Bland and Nicki Minaj situations, with many attempting to paint Bland as a belligerent Black woman resisting arrest, and Nicki as a crazed, hysterical attacker attacking the innocent Swift. Same racism, different levels, with both utilizing the 'Angry Black Girl' narrative, wherein Black women are not even allowed the autonomy to express themselves.

Racism is like an octopus with many tentacles, and the same thing that killed Sandra Bland is what we are discussing with Nicki Minaj. People have to understand that it's all the same system, and each of these instances are tentacles on the same monster.

Reading List:

1. Mokoena, Tshepo. "Taylor Swift's response to Nicki Minaj was faux-feminist and tone deaf." *The Guardian.* The Guardian. Web, July 22, 2015. <http://www.theguardian.com/music/2015/jul/22/taylor-swift-nicki-minaj-faux-feminist-tone-deaf/>.

2. Iqbal, Nosheen. "The Nicki Minaj debate is bigger than Taylor Swift's ego." *The Guardian.* The Guardian. Web, July 22, 2015. <http://www.theguardian.com/music/2015/jul/22/nicki-minaj-debate-bigger-than-taylor-swifts-ego/>.

3. Sanders, Sam. "Dashcam Video Of Sandra Bland's Arrest Released." NPR. Web. July 21, 2015. <http://www.npr.org/sections/thetwo-way/2015/07/21/425105015/dashcam-video-of-sandra-blands-arrest-released/>.

4. Yang, John, Calvin, Amy, McClam, Eric. "Sandra Bland Death: Officials Say Glitch, Not Editing, Caused Video Irregularities." NBC News. Web. July 22, 2015. <http://www.nbcnews.com/news/us-news/sandra-bland-death-officials-say-glitch-not-editing-caused-video-n396461/>.

Racism Is Like An Octopus: #BlackLivesMatter

From the day Mike Brown was killed (and even before then), our issue has been police brutality as it relates SPECIFICALLY to racism in this country. This video is going to be about the absurdity of #AllLivesMatter and my concerns regarding other protest movements hijacking the Ferguson movement to springboard their own issues into prominence.

Racism is like an octopus, and the eight legs of the octopus represent the various branches of systemic racism in the U.S. So one leg is police brutality. One leg is education/the school system, one leg is the prison system, one leg is the food desert/lack of proper nutrition, one leg is segregated neighborhoods, etc. Each leg is its own individual issue, but together they make up the larger whole of the octopus- systemic racism. A lot of people right now want to focus all their energy into cutting off the one tentacle that represents police brutality, because that's the tentacle that is currently trying to suck their faces off. But Black people understand that even once that tentacle is dead and gone, there are seven more that will still need to be dealt with. Police brutality and lethal force against Black and Brown bodies are merely SYMPTOMS of larger issues in this country, and working to end police brutality without focusing on race and racism is like merely cutting off one arm of the octopus.

Racism and anti-Blackness are woven into our society, and when you make immature and asinine comments like, 'Don't make it about race,' you are essentially saying that if we just deal with the lethal police force, there won't be any lingering racism left behind. But systemic racism is what caused these police murders in the first place; just because there have also been instances of white people being beaten by police DOES NOT NEGATE THE RACIAL IMPLICATIONS OF POLICE BRUTALITY ACROSS THE COUNTRY. There is a far bigger trend here stating that Black lives *specifically* don't matter.

When I say, 'My hair looks great today' it does NOT mean I'm saying your hair looks like shit today. So why when I say 'My BLACK LIFE MATTERS' do some of you feel like I'm saying your lives don't matter? Do you crash breast cancer rallies screaming, 'Prostate cancer matters?' No? Perhaps that's because you realize caring specifically about one thing does not inherently imply that other things are less important. People have decided they're uncomfortable with race and would rather focus on the notion of police brutality, but Black and brown bodies can't separate one from the other. WE don't have the luxury of *not* making it about race.

Police militarization and use of force IS a major issue on its own, but racism, anti-Blackness, and concepts of white supremacy play a major role in every inch of the reasoning behind why Black and brown victims are killed by police at such a higher rate than white people. Black victims are subjected to smear campaigns in the court of public opinion where they are quickly written off as 'thugs' and problems waiting to happen because of their skin color. Studies have also proven that white people feel less empathy for Black and brown bodies, view them as less innocent, more 'superhuman,' and capable of swelling up into a demonic rage that would justify six shots. None of this is prevalent in cases of police brutality involving white victims.

So don't tell me 'it's not about race' when we have created a culture of fear around Black and brown bodies that at any minute one of us could hulk out and become an immediate and imminent treat to those around us (hence why the police are called on children playing in the park or men walking with their hands in their pockets). Don't tell me this is not about race when police, security guards, or armed citizens gun down a Black person, not a WHITE person or a HISPANIC person or a NATIVE person, every 28 hours. Check out the #CrimingWhileWhite tags and #AliveWhileBlack tags and then tell me these murders were not about race. It is about race.

Imagine if you went home and your house was on fire. You called the fire department but when they arrived, they threw water on your neighbor's house instead of yours. When you asked them why they were throwing water on your neighbors house even though his house wasn't on fire, they replied, 'ALL houses matter.'

Our house is on fire. Black lives matter.

So, About That BBHMM Video...

Okay. I loved the video.

I loved the depiction of a powerful, vicious Black woman on a revenge mission with her girl gang. I loved the artistic direction, visual concepts, and storyline. (And Rih DIRECTED this herself- her creative vision is undeniable.) I loved the hair. I loved the makeup. I loved the clothes. I absolutely LOVED that it was based on her real-life drama with her accountant. [3]

But I'm petty (and y'all know this), so while watching, I couldn't help but wonder: 'Dang, I wish this was a Black girl crew.'

High-concept artistry is so often tied to 'whiteness,' and it is common for Black artists to use white people as a way of validating their work. From Basquiat not being taken seriously until he linked up with Andy Warhol to Kanye West parading around his white high-end designer friends as proof that he (and

---

[3] "Rihanna wins $10 million settlement after accountant gave her bad advice which led to her 'squandering $9m in ONE YEAR - including $7.5m on a moldy Beverly Hills mansion." The Daily Mail. The Daily Mail, February 14, 2014. Web. <http://www.dailymail.co.uk/news/article-2561519/Rihanna-settles-10-million-accountant-gave-bad-advice.html#ixzz3ekM84IPF/>

Kim) have finally been accepted into the fashion set, proximity to whiteness, (be it famous friends, clients, mentors, or fellow murderers, in Rihanna's case), is often used as a barometer for how serious we should take their artistic vision and talent (just as white people like to use proximity to Blackness as some type of 'hood pass...' here's looking at you, Miley Cyrus).

While watching Rihanna's seven-minute long video, her directorial debut, I couldn't help but think that this was a LOT of white people for what is bound to be one of her most polarizing, critically acclaimed art pieces to date. (And her music videos ARE high-concept art pieces. Let's be clear.)

I would have absolutely adored seeing a badass Black girl gang taking down these rich white motherfuckers. But I'm certain that that concept, combined with the 'trap' beat of this song, would have made people view this as nothing more than a *Black* music video and not as art. Many will see the white people in this video and that- and that ALONE- will signify to them that Rihanna is doing something hipster-ish and 'high art.' And that sucks.

But it was still fantastic.

P.S. Rihanna pissed off the white feminists with her torture and murder of a blonde white woman. So there's that. #blessed

On False Narratives and Manipulating Black Outrage

This essay is going to be about something I have noticed for awhile now, wherein people attempt to manipulate Black outrage for their own causes or agendas. The most recent example of this has been a manipulated sound bite from a recent Hillary Clinton speech, which has been floating around social media (I've seen it on both Tumblr and Twitter). The quote is out of context of the actual speech and is being used to vilify her as saying, 'Black people in hoodies are scary.' The full quote went as follows:

"...And our problem is not all kooks and Klansman. It's also in the cruel joke that goes unchallenged. It's in the off-hand comments about not wanting "those people" in the neighborhood. Let's be honest: For a lot of well-meaning, open-minded white people, the sight of a young Black man in a hoodie evokes a twinge of fear. And news reports about poverty and crime and discrimination evoke sympathy, even empathy, but too rarely do they spur us to action or prompt us to question our own assumptions and privilege."

Now, am I a Hillary fan? HELL NO.

BUT chop and screwing speeches into sound bites to create a false sense of outrage is cruel and manipulative; the same goes for editing pictures or spreading articles with incendiary titles. I noticed something similar with the circulating of a photoshopped mug shot of Sandra Bland; in it, her eyes had been whited out her eyes to further the narrative that she was already dead when the photo was taken. [4]

PSA: There is enough REAL racism out there to go around. There is no need to make up stuff to get more people riled up, or to get them to throw their weight behind your cause.

There are a lot of people out there trying to manipulate black outrage for their own personal gain, be it monetary, political, etc., and in addition to the hipster racists trolling for 'rage clicks' and reactionary outrage, you also have 'revolutionaries' and 'activists' that spread incendiary information, even if it's wrong, in order to further their cause (i.e. they don't want you to vote for Hilary so they will spread around a quote out

---

1. [4] "Sandra Bland Mugshot: 5 Fast Facts You Need to Know." *Heavy.* Heavy, July 28, 2015. Web. <http://heavy.com/news/2015/07/sandra-bland-mugshot-mug-photo-already-dead-photoshopped-edited-fake-conspiracy-theory-hoax-real-edited-photos/>

of context; or they want people to get mad about Sandra Bland so they push photo-shopped images to *prove* she was already dead when the mug shot was taken).

Again, this is cruel and manipulative.

Don't just take anyone's word for anything. (Not even mine. That's why I include a description box full of links for you guys to read and formulate your own conclusions.)

Don't just go by titles or click-bait or quotes. Don't be reactionary. Use logic. Google it, read for yourself what was actually said and done, and form and informed opinion. We are in the age of information, and there is no reason to not know what was ACTUALLY said or done. Don't be lazy, especially if you call yourself politically active. READ.

You have a brain- use it!

Reading List:

1. Young, Carla. "Trolling for Traffic: Is It Worth Tarnishing Your Brand for Clicks?" Momeo Magazine, May 15, 2012. Web. <http://www.momeomagazine.com/trolling-for-traffic-is-it-worth-tarnishing-your-brand-for-clicks/>.

2. Howley, Patrick. "Hillary: Even Open-Minded Whites Get Nervous Around Blacks In Hoodies [VIDEO]." The Daily Caller. Web. July 23, 2015. <http://dailycaller.com/2015/07/23/hillary-even-open-minded-whites-get-nervous-around-blacks-in-hoodies/#ixzz3hCsusAfg/>.

3. "Sandra Bland Mugshot: 5 Fast Facts You Need to Know." *Heavy.* Heavy, July 28, 2015. Web. <http://heavy.com/news/2015/07/sandra-bland-mugshot-mug-photo-already-dead-photoshopped-edited-fake-conspiracy-theory-hoax-real-edited-photos/>.

'Go Back To Your Country' RANT

Let's rant, shall we?

White folks are the only people that can force other people to assimilate into their culture and then accuse them of appropriation.

"If you don't like it, go back to Africa."

First of all, this is not your country. Why do we have to leave? You first. Go back to Europe and give this country back to the natives.

Second of all, send us home for FREE and I'll think about it! My people were brought here for free, worked to the bone building this country for free, why should I have to pay to go back to Africa.

And stop whining about how minorities use *your* things.

"You drive in our cars."

The 'Big Three' motor companies were all started pre-Integration: General Motors in 1908, Ford in 1903, and Chrysler in 1925[5]. Black people did have our own transport companies at

---

[5] Big Three (automobile manufacturers): https://en.m.wikipedia.org/wiki/Big_Three_(automobile_ma nufacturers)

this time; maybe if we hadn't been forced to integrate, we WOULD have our own big motor companies. But white supremacy has enabled huge, white-owned corporations to thrive while turning Black people into glorified consumers. Maybe you shouldn't be so proud of that.

And the funniest part is, the vast majority of the things white people lay claim to was actually invented or assisted by POC; we just learn revisionist, white supremacist, Eurocentric curriculum that brainwashes us into believing that white contributions to the world vastly overshadow that of POC. But if you dig deep enough behind almost every modern invention, you will find a person of color.

From J. Marion Sims[6], known as the father of modern gynecology, who based his entire work around experimentation on slaves, to George Otto Gey[7], the scientist credited with creating the first immortal stem cell line, which he harvested from a Black woman, Henrietta Lacks[8], without her consent.

---

[6] J. Marion Sims (Wikipedia)
https://en.wikipedia.org/wiki/J._Marion_Sims

[7] George Otto Gey (Wikipedia):
https://en.m.wikipedia.org/wiki/George_Otto_Gey

Revisionist white history has enabled white people to steal from POC without consequences. It has enabled white people to force POC to speak their language, assimilate into their culture, wipe out entire races, annihilate entire cultures, force us to learn your European ways and customs- then act as if, not only did you do us a favor, but as if POC had a choice in the matter. Like it was something we wanted to do.

Come on, white people. Do better.

---

[8] Henrietta Lacks (Wikipedia): https://en.m.wikipedia.org/wiki/Henrietta_Lacks

Reading List

1. Zimmerman, Neetzan. "Principal Bans Hispanic Students from Speaking Spanish." Gawker. Web. December 4, 2013. <http://gawker.com/principal-bans-hispanic-students-from-speaking-spanish-1476714515/>.

2. Taborn, Tyrone D. "A Black Man Invented The PC As We Know It Today..." W.E. A.L.L. B.E. Blog. Web. October 9, 2007. <http://weallbe.blogspot.com/2007/10/black-man-invented-pc-as-we-know-it.html?m=1/>.

3. Henrietta Lacks (Wikipedia): https://en.m.wikipedia.org/wiki/Henrietta_Lacks

4. HeLa (Wikipedia): https://en.m.wikipedia.org/wiki/HeLa

5. George Otto Gey (Wikipedia): https://en.m.wikipedia.org/wiki/George_Otto_Gey

6. Big Three (automobile manufacturers): https://en.m.wikipedia.org/wiki/Big_Three_(automobile manufacturers)

7. Mark Dean (computer scientist): https://en.m.wikipedia.org/wiki/Mark_Dean_(computer scientist)

8. J. Marion Sims (Wikipedia): https://en.wikipedia.org/wiki/J._Marion_Sims

So, About Black Academics and the Great white Fraud (Rachel Dolezal)...

This essay is going to revolve around Black academia/elitism, white femininity, and respectability politics.

I think that a lot of the defense that we are still seeing, even as this woman's story has unraveled, has to do with the fact that she is not just a white person, with white privilege, but that she is also a white WOMAN and an academic. Many people, Black and white, see her as a delicate thing to be protected; as pure, innocent, childlike, and completely unaware of her actions. (This is reflected in language being used to defend her, like calling her detractors 'mean.')

white femininity is rooted in concepts of innocence and purity, so it is not surprising that many people have adopted the stance of, 'She's not so bad,' 'She didn't know what she was doing,' and 'Black people are just being mean to her.' Black/white racism in this country is often framed around Black male + white male relations, while the racism of white woman is often swept under the rug or explained away under the guise, 'She is a woman, so it can't be that bad.'

People are also utilizing her 'good work' and association with the NAACP as a way to excuse her lies, as if her being an academic somehow balances the scales. While youth leaders and other organizers not affiliated with recognized orgs or movements CONSTANTLY have to prove themselves to get their work recognized, this white woman gets the benefit of the doubt because she is affiliated with certain 'respectable' orgs and schools. This is respectability politics. She does NOT automatically get a pass because she works for an institution that you have heard of; even respectable institutions/workers make mistakes, can be wrong, or can be bad people.

Lastly, I think a lot of Black academics and elites are hesitant to challenge her *Blackness* because, on a lot of levels, they identify with her. Many of these people went to the same schools as her, attended the same classes as her, went on to join the same organizations as her, and even do the same work as her. It is clear that many of these Black people who are defending her, and who are having difficulty even challenging her, feel like to challenge her 'Blackness' would be to challenge their own Blackness.

Many of the concepts of Black academia and Black elitism revolve around white supremacy and approximation to whiteness. They go to certain schools, get certain jobs, and live in certain neighborhoods, all as a way to ascertain their closeness to white people and, by extension, their own self-worth. These people are suffering from internalized racism, anti-blackness, and inferiority complexes.

Many Black academics have often also felt disconnected from the Black community (due to stereotypes that intelligence and greatness are 'white' things), so they look at an accomplished white woman in blackface and they see themselves in her, and her in them. They have truly bought, 100%, into ideas of white supremacy, and they spend their whole academic lives trying to escape stereotypical *blackness* and redefine it.

And doesn't that sound familiar?

Reading List

1. Deliovs, Katerina. *White Femininity: Race, Gender & Power.* Ontario: Fernwood Publishing Co., Ltd. 2010. <http://www.amazon.com/White-Femininity-Race-Gender-Power/dp/1552663523/>.

2. Deliovsky, Kathy. "Normative White Femininity: Race, Gender and the Politics of Beauty." *Atlantis: Critical Studies in Gender, Culture & Social Justice/Études critiques sur le genre, la culture, et la justice.* Web. (pdf) n.d. <http://journals.msvu.ca/index.php/atlantis/article/view/429/422/.>

So, About That NAACP President, Rachel Dolezal...

This essay is going to be about Rachel Dolezal, the president of the NAACP's Spokane, Washington chapter, and a white woman who has been 'passing' for Black for at least the last six years[9]. Becoming enamored with Black culture after her (white) parents adopted Black children, she garnered multiple degrees in African-American studies before moving to Spokane, Washington.

A virtual unknown in Spokane, Dolezal set about reinventing herself as a Black woman, darkening her skin, changing her hair, and self-identifying as Black. She also created an elaborate backstory about her family and upbringing, which included allegations of abuse against her parents so no one would dig too deeply into her family, past, or home life.

Dolezal used her faux Blackness as a way to break into activism and politics, teaching classes on African-American Studies; in addition to teaching, she eventually worked her way up to President of the NAACP chapter. Many, however, suspected

---

[9] Herbst, Diane. "Inside Story: How Rachel Dolezal's Cover as a Black Woman Was Blown." People Magazine. People, June 20, 2015. Web. <http://www.people.com/article/rachel-dolezal-black-woman-cover-blown-hate-crimes/>.

something was off, especially when Dolezal was the recipient of several untraceable 'hate' packages. Believing she had possibly sent them to herself and that she was not actually Black, a local newspaper contacted her biological family, who revealed the truth: she had been born a Caucasian woman.

This woman is clearly disturbed.

I am not of the mindset that 'Imitation is the sincerest form of flattery,' and anyone that has taken a basic 'Racism 101' class should understand cultural appropriation and why it's problematic. There has also been some really annoying chatter about how if 'Black women are allowed to try to be white, then white women should be allowed to try to be Black.' This is a false equivalence that does not take into account how Black women grow up in a white supremacist society that pushes Eurocentric beauty ideals. We don't literally want to be white; we have just been conditioned to think whiteness is beautiful. This woman literally wanted to be Black.

She has been occupying Black female spaces while in blackface, and she was utilizing and appropriating Black culture and experiences in order to further her career and occupy Black revolutionary spaces. There is a perversion to that. Although she has accomplished much in the Black community, it is viciously undercut by the fact that she did it not as herself, but as a white woman in blackface.

There have been white NAACP leaders in the past; there have even been militant pro-black white allies like John Brown. Everything she accomplished could have been accomplished without pretending to be Black. She just wanted to be Black SO BAD that she created this false racial identity (based off of caricatures) and committed to it.

As much as she knows about *being black* aka Black stereotypes, as much as she has educated herself on Black struggle or Black culture, as much as she has done for the Black community, she is not Black and will never be Black. She always has the option of going home, washing that lacquer off her skin, taking off that weave, and picking up her whiteness again if she feels like it. That is a crucial distinction to make, and one that proves the inherent issue with 'ethnicity identity;' similar to cultural appropriation, it is always in the favor of the dominant ethnicity.

It's not about saying, 'Well, why can't we just be whatever we want?' because this mindset is not even POSSIBLE without a certain amount of privilege. As we saw in McKinney, whiteness is invisible. But to Black people and other POC, race is not some abstract concept; it is a solid marker of our identities. Black people never get to stop being Black. We NEVER get to say, 'You know what, I choose to ethnically identify as white today, so cops please stop profiling/harassing/killing me.'

Black people DON'T get to identify ourselves and live the lives we choose. We are constantly trying to navigate in hostile, oppressive spaces under white supremacy, and white people CONSTANTLY think they can cherry pick the *fun* parts of a Black racial/ethnic identity without having to deal with any of that pesky racism and oppression. We don't have that luxury. We don't have that PRIVILEGE. We're Black through the good and the bad, and we can't pick an 'ethnic identity.' We were born Black into a society and a world, really, that sees Blackness as an issue, and we can't just choose to ethnically identify as something else and opt out of systemic oppression and racism.

Reading List

1. Herbst, Diane. "Inside Story: How Rachel Dolezal's Cover as a Black Woman Was Blown." *People Magazine.* People, June 20, 2015. Web. <http://www.people.com/article/rachel-dolezal-black-woman-cover-blown-hate-crimes/>.

On Relationships and Dating

Let me warn you now: a lot of people are not going to like what I have to say in this essay.

I do not subscribe to any type of 'war' between black men and black women.

As far as dating and relationships go, it's hard out here for everybody; however, similar to the concept of 'black on black crime,' there is a racial element injected into BM/BW dating scenarios that we do not see anywhere else.

What I mean by that is, marriage rates as a whole in this country are down, [10] divorce rates are up, and people of all races are waiting later to get married. You also have a whole media genre (romantic comedy i.e. 'rom com') built around dating and relationship woes, and it's very common to see certain concepts in movies and shows about dating: for example, women are nags, women only like jocks or rich guys, or 'it's hard to find a good man.'

---

[10] Demby, Gene. "Marriage Rates Are Falling, And For Some Faster Than Others." NPR. Web. September 26, 2014. <http://www.npr.org/sections/codeswitch/2014/09/26/35 1736134/marriage-rates-are-falling-and-for-some-faster-than-ohters/>.

Shows/movies like *Sex and the City*, *10 Things I Hate About You*, and *She's All That*, are built entirely around some of these concepts without any interjection of race; yet we see black people fling racialized versions of these same stereotypes/concepts at one another, stating 'All BLACK women want jocks/rich men;' 'All BLACK women are nags;' or, 'It's hard to find a good BLACK man.'

A lot of Black people are suffering from internalized racism so they buy into and perpetuate stereotypes and self hate introduced to them by a white supremacist media. You also have Black people that want to date each other but are so invested in these stereotypes and concepts that have been fed to them that they believe in that more than actual reality, and they create this idea in their mind that it's absolutely IMPOSSIBLE to date another Black person or that switching to another race is somehow 'the answer."

But people are people and dating is dating. There is no magic pill to make dating work, especially not dating interracially, because ALL relationships require work to overcome problems like nagging, attitudes, getting on each other's nerves, and trust.

If you aren't finding what you want out there, you have two options:

1. Expand your circle. Look for people in different places; stop doing the same thing and expecting different results (i.e. stop going out to the club, meeting club girls, then getting upset when they want to club. Stop meeting guys in the same shady spots, and then getting surprised when all they want is to have sex).

2. Work on yourself. If you have expanded your circle and things still aren't working out, look within. Work on yourself so that you are the best person you can be when and if 'The One' comes along.

Don't be desperate to find someone or being overly concerned about being companionless; it is perfectly fine to be companionless until you find what you want. Meet people and let relationships happen organically. If you know you want to date a black man/woman, only date Black people. Don't have it in the back of your head that the relationship probably won't work out or that you will switch to other races, because then you will find yourself using those excuses as an exit strategy when things get difficult or as a way to settle for something you really don't want. (For example, switching to white people because you 'can't find' a Black person is a cop out; there are MILLIONS of Black people in the world and you can't have literally dated every single one).

Dating is hard. And Black people suffer from additional issues with internalized racism that make us hate each another. But we have been tricked and brainwashed into believing something that's simply not true; there ARE good Black men out there, there ARE good Black women out there, and if you want to date a Black man or a Black women, get out there and DATE! If all you're seeing is negativity towards Black women from BM and vice versa, cut that crap out of your life. Expand your dating pool, work on yourself, and don't settle. It will happen.

Reading List

1. Demby, Gene. "Marriage Rates Are Falling, And For Some Faster Than Others." NPR. Web. September 26, 2014. <http://www.npr.org/sections/codeswitch/2014/09/26/351736134/marriage-rates-are-falling-and-for-some-faster-than-ohters/>.

2. Bedard, Paul. "Census: Marriage rate at 93-year low, even including same-sex couples." *The Washington Examiner.* Washington Examiner, September 18, 2014. Web. <http://www.washingtonexaminer.com/census-marriage-rate-at-93-year-low-even-including-same-sex-couples/article/2553600/>.

3. Wang, Wendy, Parker, Kim. "Record Share of Americans Have Never Married." Pew Research Center. Web. September 24, 2014. <http://www.pewsocialtrends.org/2014/09/24/record-share-of-americans-have-never-married/>.

4. Desmond-Harris, Jenee. "Myth-Busting the Black Marriage 'Crisis.'" The Root. Web. August 18, 2011. <http://www.theroot.com/articles/culture/2011/08/black_marriage_good_news_by_the_numbers.html/>.

Black on Black Crime Is A Myth (REALLY, It Is!)

Black on Black crime is not a thing. And I am sick to death of people pretending it is.

Blacks do not kill a disproportionate amount of other Black people.

Blacks do not kill a disproportionate amount of other Black people.

Blacks do not kill a disproportionate amount of other Black people.

Blacks do not kill a disproportionate amount of other Black people.

Blacks do not kill a disproportionate amount of other Black people.

All crime is related to race and neighborhood, aka the majority of violent crimes are committed by members of the same race against other members of the same race, and typically by people that live in the same neighborhood (and people of the same race tend to congregate together and live near each other). The rates of violent crimes committed by Black people against other Black people is 92%, the rates of violent crimes committed by white people against other white people is 84%, and so and so forth with other races (Hispanics kill Hispanics, Asians kill Asians, etc.). Blacks are not more or less violent than any other race; however, studies have shown that the media OVER-REPORTS Black crime more than any other race (at a margin of 30%. THIRTY PERCENT). Black-on Black crime is actually at the lowest it's been in ten years (thanks to programs like My Brother's Keeper[11] and the Question Bridge Initiative[12]), while white on white crime is actually on the upswing.

Crime (and even violent crime) is a normal part of society; whites kill each other all the time and it is not news. Blacks don't even commit the most violent crimes or drug-related offenses in this country, white people do. But Blacks are disproportionately reported on in the media for crime as well as being jailed disproportionately for violent crime and drug offenses, which statistically are more common amongst white people.

Wake up. Black on Black crime is a myth.

---

[11] https://www.whitehouse.gov/my-brothers-keeper

[12] http://questionbridge.com

The myth of Black on Black crime was created by white supremacy as a way to keep Black people distracted from racial injustice enacted on us by white people. All crime is proportionate to race and neighborhood; i.e. whites kill whites, Asians kill Asians, etc. And notice how incidents of 'white on white crime,' like the recent Waco, TX incident that left 9 dead and 18 injured, are never referred to as such. They are never grouped under the umbrella of racial crime nor are they seen as indications of a larger social problem within the white community.

The vast majority of crime is INTRA-racial (between members of the same racial group) and not INTER-racial. Black people do not kill a disproportionate number of other Black people. BUT even if we did (which we don't), examining the reasons behind crime in Black neighborhoods goes back to underlying problems in our communities caused by white supremacy: lack of jobs or educational opportunities, forced to live in impoverished ghettos, and instilled with a sense of worthlessness. I am sick and tired of people parroting this rhetoric about 'Black on Black crime' with no critical understanding of the real issues. We love to talk about how Black people are crabs in a bucket- but a crab's natural habitat is not a bucket!

We will do anything to survive in this bucket.

Reading List

1. Azrael, Kush. "Report: white on white crime rate exceeds that of black on black crime." Black Youth Project. Web. August 18, 2014. <http://www.blackyouthproject.com/2014/08/report-white-on-white-crime-rate-exceeds-that-of-black-on-black-crime/>.

2. Yglesias, Matthew. "White-on-white murder in America is out of control." *Vox.* Vox, February 20, 2015. Web. < http://www.vox.com/2014/8/21/6053811/white-on-white-murder/>.

3. Coddett, Kerry. "White on White Crime: An Unspoken Tragedy." *Black Voices*, The Huffington Post. Web. March 2, 2015. <http://www.huffingtonpost.com/kerry-coddett/white-on-white-crime-an-u_b_6771878.html/>.

4. Williams, Edward Wyckoff. "Don't White People Kill Each Other, Too?" *The Root.* Web, April 10, 2012. <http://www.theroot.com/articles/culture/2012/04/whiteon white_crime_it_goes_against_the_false_media_narrative.h tml/.

5. Jackson, Michael. "The Myth of the Black on Black Crime Epidemic." Demos. Web. July 29, 2013. <http://www.demos.org/blog/7/29/13/myth-black-black-crime-epidemic/>.

6. Mirkinson, Jack. "Study's Disturbing Findings About How The Media Covers Race And Crime." *HuffPost Media,* The Huffington Post. Web. August 28, 2014. <http://www.huffingtonpost.com/2014/08/28/media-black-crime-rates_n_5728780.html/>.

7. Gedeon, Kimberly. "PERCEPTION ISN'T REALITY: SLANTED NEWS COVERAGE OF BLACKS PERPETUATES DANGEROUS RACIAL STEREOTYPES." Madame Noire. Web. August 26, 2014.

<http://madamenoire.com/462799/perception-isnt-reality-slanted-news-coverage-blacks-perpetuates-dangerous-racial-stereotypes/>.

8. Prince, Richard. "How Media Have Shaped Our Perceptions On Race and Crime." *The Root.* Web. September 4, 2014. <http://www.theroot.com/blogs/journalisms/2014/09/how_media_have_shaped_our_perception_of_race_and_crime.html/>.

9. Dowler, Kenneth. "MEDIA CONSUMPTION AND PUBLIC ATTITUDES TOWARD CRIME AND JUSTICE: THE RELATIONSHIP BETWEEN FEAR OF CRIME, PUNITIVE ATTITUDES, AND PERCEIVED POLICE EFFECTIVENESS." *Journal of Criminal Justice and Popular Culture.* Department of Criminal Justice, California State University at Bakersfield. Web. n.d. http://www.albany.edu/scj/jcjpc/vol10is2/dowler.html/>.

On 'Mad Max,' Blind Spots, and white Supremacist Fantasies

I am so tired of hearing about how great 'Mad Max: Fury Road' is. [13]

Because all I can think about whenever I see a trailer for it is how WHITE 'Mad Max: Fury Road' is.

The post-apocalyptic juggernaut being heralded as an 'instant pulp classic,' features an overwhelmingly white cast (Zoe Kravitz is the lone Black person with a name or speaking role), despite the fact that it is set in an entirely fictitious future (perhaps a version of Australia, as in previous Mad Max installments). Lots of glowing reviews have named the lack of diversity as something merely 'regrettable,' but 'easily overlooked' because of how great the movie is.

It's easy to overlook lack of representation of marginalized groups when you're represented; it's much more difficult to ignore lack of representation when you are part of the marginalized group. Even when you enjoy the content, it's not so easy to just overlook lack of diversity, and it is always the marginalized group

---

[13] Orr, Christopher. "Diary of a Madman." *The Atlantic.* May 15, 2015. Web.
<http://www.theatlantic.com/entertainment/archive/2015/05/fury-road/393353/>.

being asked to 'take one for the team,' and place content quality over representation. This is a microaggression and it happens again and again within our largely white media system.

I'm not saying EVERY story has to include racial minorities (an accusation I often hear from white fandoms), but when *universal* and *all-encompassing,* 'voice of a generation' stories set in some of the most diverse cities in the world (like New York or Los Angeles) are CONSISTENTLY all White, there is a problem. There is a message being sent that racial minorities don't exist and we don't matter.

When post-apocalyptic, end of the world stories like 'Mad Max' or 'Zombieland' are consistently all White or majority White, they send the message that POC don't make it through the apocalypse. And when futuristic sci-fi stories like 'Her' are consistently all white, they send the message that white people just don't see us in the future, plain and simple. (Similar messages are sent with the refusal to feature Black people, and especially Black women, in superhero films- we are just not 'super.')

We have seen these types of stories done successfully with diverse casts ('Book of Eli,' 'Demolition Man,' 'Firefly/Serenity,' and '28 Days Later' all come to mind), so at this point, lack of racial diversity in speculative fiction honestly feels like a very deliberate slap in the face. However, I do believe that much of it comes from the blind spots formed when every level of production on a film or other media creation is all White. white people don't think about racial diversity in speculative fiction because they largely don't think about race. But that doesn't change the fact that these are white supremacist fantasies, period; perpetuating white fantasy worlds where people of color simply do not exist.

And that's just unacceptable.

Reading List

1. Orr, Christopher. "Diary of a Madman." *The Atlantic.* May 15, 2015. Web. <http://www.theatlantic.com/entertainment/archive/2015/05/fury-road/393353/>.

2. Geekonius, Darth. "Does 'Mad Max' Have A Diversity Problem?" The Black Geeks. May 12, 2015. Web. <http://theblackgeeks.com/does-mad-max-have-a-diversity-problem/>.

3. Berlatsky, Noah. "Star Wars and the 4 Ways Science Fiction Handles Race." *The Atlantic.* March 25, 2014. Web. <http://www.theatlantic.com/entertainment/archive/2014/03/-em-star-wars-em-and-the-4-ways-science-fiction-handles-race/359507/>.

IS The White Man's Ice Actually Colder? On Black People and Larry Bird Syndrome

There has been a big kerfuffle being made about a 'reformed' white redneck posting anti-racist videos on YouTube[14]; while I think this is commendable (because, as I've said before, racism is white people problem and nothing will change until THEY address it, they need to handle their own problems instead of worrying about Black people all the time), I find it disconcerting the amount of support/attention he's getting from Black people. The same people that said we shouldn't be protesting or claimed, 'there is no race problem,' will now be amazed that a white person has admitted it.

Black folks will ignore or put down something another Black person says, but as soon as a white person says it they will fall all over themselves to agree; this is because we are conditioned to think white people are naturally better/smarter/etc. than us. They're NOT.

---

[14] Kabas, Marisa. "This Reformed Redneck Is Sending white People A Wake-Up Call About Racism." *The Daily Dot.* Daily Dot, April 10, 2015. Web. <http://www.dailydot.com/lifestyle/reformed-redneck-dixon-white-racism/>.

This is commonly referred to as 'Larry Bird syndrome[15],' wherein white people enter into traditionally Black/POC spaces and get awards, attention, and accolades thrown at them for being amazing and wonderful and revolutionary- when they are really JUST existing as white in a Black or POC space (which makes them unique). They're an anomaly, a gimmick that is supported by white as well as black people. Whites will always push one of their own because they prefer EVERYTHING to come from a White face, and many Blacks agree- we take it as a *compliment* when whites show interest in and excel at 'Black' things or when they agree with our theories and ideas (such as the reformed redneck utilizing anti-racist rhetoric). There is an implication that whites are superior to us, so we should be flattered that they're interested in our lowly Black activities. We think that white validation somehow gives credibility to our ideas (and music, and dances, and talent, and WHATEVER else). We have been

---

[15] Johnson, Roy S. "THOMAS EXPLAINS COMMENTS ON BIRD." *The New York Times.* Special to the New York Times, June 5, 1987. Web. <http://www.nytimes.com/1987/06/05/sports/thomas-explains-comments-on-bird.html/>.

conditioned to be black white supremacists. There is an unconscious bias within us that black people are inferior.

This all started with Black youth activists in Ferguson, and has been spearheaded by Black activists for the past YEAR. This white dude opens his mouth for less than a month and I'm seeing articles headlined with, 'White Man Starts Race Revolution[16],' despite the fact that he isn't saying anything that Black and POC activists haven't been saying for MONTHS.

Black folks need to STOP entertaining and going along with this notion that our own words, ideas, thoughts, and theories are better coming from a non-Black person. white people are not better than you and you don't need them to regurgitate your own ideas back to you before you believe it.

---

[16] Morris, Randa. "This 'Redneck' May Have Just Started A White Revolution Against Racism (VIDEO)." Addicting Info. Web. April 11, 2015.
<http://www.addictinginfo.org/2015/04/11/this-redneck-may-have-just-started-a-white-revolution-against-racism-video/>.

Reading List

1. Kabas, Marisa. "This Reformed Redneck Is Sending white People A Wake-Up Call About Racism." *The Daily Dot.* Daily Dot, April 10, 2015. Web. <http://www.dailydot.com/lifestyle/reformed-redneck-dixon-white-racism/>.

2. Morris, Randa. "This 'Redneck' May Have Just Started A White Revolution Against Racism (VIDEO)." Addicting Info. Web. April 11, 2015. <http://www.addictinginfo.org/2015/04/11/this-redneck-may-have-just-started-a-white-revolution-against-racism-video/>.

3. Johnson, Roy S. "THOMAS EXPLAINS COMMENTS ON BIRD." *The New York Times.* Special to the New York Times, June 5, 1987. Web. <http://www.nytimes.com/1987/06/05/sports/thomas-explains-comments-on-bird.html/>.

On Black Women and Respectability Politics

Women, and especially Black women, have to live our daily lives according to a certain set of rules on what makes us 'respectable' or not, and it is especially difficult when dealing with both racism and sexism. Singer Janelle Monae has sent long-term fans into a tizzy with her most recent song and video, 'Yoga[17];' in the video, she wears tight jeans and yoga pants, and espouses lyrics about 'posing and flexing,' a far cry from her previously non-conformist messages and outfit of suit and saddle shoes.

On a parallel, rapper Wale painted a portrait of three young women single and living life through a drug-fueled, social media fog in the video for his song, 'Girls on Drugs[18],' that came out the same week as Monae's single; however, it was an imperfect image that posed the young Black women as shallow

---

[17] Bitchie, Necole. "[Get Off My Areola!] Janelle Monae Breaks It Down In New 'Yoga' Video." Necole Bitchie blog. Web. April 13, 2015. <http://necolebitchie.com/2015/04/janelle-monae-goes-sexy-in-new-video-yoga/#ixzz3XJ21zjIl/>.

[18] Fleischer, Adam. "Wale Tells A Cautionary Tale In His 'The Girls On Drugs' Video." *MTV News*. MTV, April 13, 2015. Web. <http://www.mtv.com/news/2132066/wale-the-girls-on-drugs-video/>.

and self-absorbed without any real critique of the culture and society that glorifies and glamorizes such lifestyles. Wale's video also didn't show any excessively self-destructive behavior (it was FAR from Rihanna's, 'We Found Love,' for example) and came off more or less as a preachy morality tale about what happens to 'bad girls' that don't stay home every night. (And lyrics like, 'I'm looking for a real woman but she just wants to be wild' only further this point.)

Black women do not have to play games of respectability politics to deserve or garner respect. Janelle Monae is a talented, accomplished artist regardless of whether or not she is singing in yoga pants or a full suit; and while there is a discussion to be had about the effects of drug abuse and social media on a fame-hungry society, bashing individual women instead of examine the context of how they got there is not the way to go about it. Not to mention, there is nothing INHERENTLY wrong with young women going out, having fun, or even occasionally engaging in drugs and/or alcohol. Women, and especially Black women, are held to an impossible standard of things we have to say or do in order to be seen as 'respectable.' Just as I encourage people not to engage to race-respectability politics to be seen as human beings worthy of respect, women don't have to do it, either.

Reading List

1. Bitchie, Necole. "[Get Off My Areola!] Janelle Monae Breaks It Down In New 'Yoga' Video." Necole Bitchie blog. Web. April 13, 2015. <http://necolebitchie.com/2015/04/janelle-monae-goes-sexy-in-new-video-yoga/#ixzz3XJ21zjIl/>.

2. Fleischer, Adam. "Wale Tells A Cautionary Tale In His 'The Girls On Drugs' Video." *MTV News.* MTV, April 13, 2015. Web. <http://www.mtv.com/news/2132066/wale-the-girls-on-drugs-video/>.

PSA: No One Is Questioning Your Blackness

I'm exhausted from talking about colorism at this point.

So I was having a conversation with someone on colorism this morning, and the concept of pointing out light privilege = questioning Blackness came into play. When I mentioned that I found this to be a strange and confusing concept, the person I was talking to basically said that many light-skinned people equate Blackness with struggle and oppression, and so when you say they have privilege, they feel you are taking away from their struggle- aka you are taking away from their Blackness.

I was shocked. Privilege comes in all manner of adjectives (thin privilege, male privilege, and pretty privilege all immediately come to mind), and none of those forms take away the essence of who a person is. To me, if you're Black, you're Black, and no one can take your Blackness away. Diving deeper into the issue, I came to the conclusion that the real problem many lighter-complexioned Black people have is not that someone is questing their Blackness by pointing out that their struggle (or lack thereof) is different than a dark-skinned person, but that the burden of the guilt they feel over being light enough to have privilege in the first place causes them to lash out and attempt to deflect people from talking about their privilege. They are in a state of denial because they don't WANT to have benefited from slavery.

The feelings of guilt and shame over having a privilege that one didn't earn are understandable, but denying it with cries of, 'We are all the same!' or 'This is divisive' doesn't lessen the impact of light privilege or make it go away. Lighter skinned people need to be able to say, "Yes, I am Black, but I do recognize that I have light privilege. I accept it and will work to check my privilege and hold myself and others accountable." This does not have anything to do with struggling more or less, or being more less or less Black (especially in the eyes of white people, who may give light-skinned people privileges but STILL recognize that they are Black) but rather, with recognizing that we live in a racist, white supremacist and Eurocentric society that has placed an inordinate amount of importance on skin color. We are all Black, but all our Black is not equal.

PSA: No one is questioning your Blackness.

PSA: Celebrity Commentary Matters

This is a PSA I have wanted to write for a while, but especially after the comments we've heard from rappers Common and A$AP Ferg[19]. The two gave their (asinine) opinions on race and were promptly taken to task by Black social media, but anytime Black celebrities make ignorant statements such as these, there is also inevitably a second crowd of people that come out of the woodwork screaming about how celebrities 'aren't Civil Rights Leaders,' and how we 'shouldn't look to celebrities for opinions on race.' While this is fine and dandy on a personal level (because certainly no one can force you to personally care about a celebrity opinion), it is silly and dismissive on a larger scale to not comprehend the amount of power and influence these celebrities really have. I also find the erasure of Black celebrity involvement in the Civil Rights Movement to be extremely interesting, as there was a time when MANY Black celebrities used their platforms to speak out on racial issues.[20]

---

[19] Callahan, Yesha. "This Week, Two Rappers Proved They Know Nothing About Racism and Live in Imaginary Post-Racial Worlds." The Root. Web. March 20, 2015. <http://www.theroot.com/blogs/the_grapevine/2015/03/this_week_rappers_proved_they_know_nothing_about_racism_live_in_imaginary.html/>.

In the age of social media, celebrities have a platform that allows their comments to reach MILLIONS of people. Regardless of how you may PERSONALLY feel about that reach, it is real and it is there. They have the ability to reach and influence millions of people- have you ever heard of product endorsements? It is the same concept, wherein brands pay celebrities to hawk a product because of their INFLUENCE. Do not pretend that ignorant comments made by a celebrity does have the ability to reach millions of people or to impact lives.

Many people like to scoff at the concept of celebrities influencing youth, but this is an anthropological truth: at a certain age, we all begin to be molded and influenced no longer by our parents, but by our peers and the media we consume- which includes our favorite artists. This is a concept that people find it easy to understand when we're talking about diversity and representation (and why diverse representation matters- it has an IMPACT), but somehow fail to grasp when discussing the

---

[20] Raymond, Emilie. "Stars for Freedom: Hollywood, Black Celebrities, and the Civil Rights Movement." Online video clip. *YouTube*. YouTube, Jun 24, 2015. Web. < https://www.youtube.com/watch?v=0NSy_dERbYk/>.

negative impact of ignorant racial statements made by Black

celebrities.

PSA: Celebrity commentary matters.

Reading List

1. Callahan, Yesha. "This Week, Two Rappers Proved They Know Nothing About Racism and Live in Imaginary Post-Racial Worlds." The Root. Web. March 20, 2015. <http://www.theroot.com/blogs/the_grapevine/2015/03/this_week_rappers_proved_they_know_nothing_about_racism_live_in_imaginary.html/>.

2. de Guzman, Maria R.T. "Friendships, Peer Influence, and Peer Pressure During the Teen Years." NebGuide. University of Nebraska-Lincoln Extension, Institute of Agriculture and Natural Resources. Web. n.d. <http://www.ianrpubs.unl.edu/epublic/pages/publicationD.jsp?publicationId=837/>.

3. Paton, Graeme. "Children 'learn most from peers not parents." *The Telegraph.* Web. April 26, 2007. < http://www.telegraph.co.uk/news/uknews/1549711/Children-learn-most-from-peers-not-parents.html/>.

4. Raymond, Emilie. "Stars for Freedom: Hollywood, Black Celebrities, and the Civil Rights Movement." Online video clip. *YouTube.* YouTube, Jun 24, 2015. Web. < https://www.youtube.com/watch?v=0NSy_dERbYk/>.

So, About That Common Interview with Jon Stewart...

Go ahead and add another one to the New Black list.

Rapper Common recently weighed in with his thoughts about racism on 'The Daily Show' with Jon Stewart, and in a series of controversial statements, he claimed Black people need to 'extend a hand in love' to white people in order to end racism[21], and likened Black/white race relations to a love relationship:

"I'm not sitting there like 'white people y'all did us wrong.' I mean we know that that existed. I don't need to keep bringing that up. It's like being in a relationship and continue to bring up the person's issues... Now I'm saying 'Hey, I love you. Let's move past this. Come on baby lets get past this."

Wow. It's a classic case of victim blaming[22] to make the burden of ending racism the responsibility of Black people, who have historically been the oppressed and not the oppressor.

---

[21] Causey, James E. "Common's way to end racism." Uncommon Causey. The Milwaukee-Wisconsin Journal Sentinel, March 17, 2015. Web. <http://www.jsonline.com/blogs/news/296619201.html/>.

[22] "Victim Blaming." The Canadian Resource Centre for Victims of Crime. The Canadian Resource Centre for Victims of Crime . August 2009. Web. <http://crcvc.ca/docs/victim_blaming.pdf/>.

Victim blaming occurs when the victim of a crime or any wrongful act is held entirely or partially responsible for the harm that befell them, and, for the millionth time, Black people are not responsible for white behavior. 'Race' as a construct was created by white people, as were the systems that enable racism and allow white supremacy to perpetuate itself in this country. There is literally NOTHING Black people can do to change the mind of a white racist, because they hate us for a purely illogical reason: our skin color.

Only when white people acknowledge the trauma of slavery and segregation, the long-term effects that racist institutions have had on our country and it's inhabitants, and begin to put in the work themselves to end it, can we move forward from racism.

Reading List

1. Causey, James E. "Common's way to end racism."
    Uncommon Causey. *The Milwaukee-Wisconsin Journal
    Sentinel,* March 17, 2015. Web.
    <http://www.jsonline.com/blogs/news/296619201.html/>.

2. "Victim Blaming." *The Canadian Resource Centre for
    Victims of Crime.* The Canadian Resource Centre for
    Victims of Crime . August 2009. Web.
    <http://crcvc.ca/docs/victim_blaming.pdf/>.

PSA: Just Because You're A POC Doesn't Mean You're Not Anti-Black (On Black Visibility)

This PSA is based off of a comment I received on my 'white Girl With Box Braids RANT' video, wherein a Hispanic/Latin@ girl asked me why I had to focus *specifically* on white appropriation of Black culture when other races suffer from cultural appropriation as well. She wanted to get into an 'Oppression Olympics-esque' argument about who was MORE oppressed, and accused me of 'not caring' about the oppression of other races.

I replied that I'm Black and can really only speak for myself and not others; not to mention the fact that the video was in fact about a very specific Black/white issue. I told her that if she didn't like me talking about Black issues then she could feel free to watch another person, or, even better, to make their own videos! (I watch videos all the time from people of other races that don't make me feel excluded but instead, inspire me to make a similar video from my own Black perspective.) What's the point of leaving an angry comment about how a person did not address your marginalized group?? Why WOULD they or SHOULD they?

The real kicker here is that this person absolutely LOVED my other videos! Only the one where I talk about Black people SPECIFICALLY triggered a very visceral and negative reaction. Why? Why do non-Black people feel so offended by Black visibility, and why does it act as the catalyst for a driving need to make Black issues about themselves?

There is a common lament against the specificity of discussing Black topics, claiming that it is 'exclusionary;' however, this pushback against specificity ONLY occurs when we are talking about Black visibility. No one pushes back against the specificity of walking for breast cancer or dumping ice over your head for ALS; there is an understanding that caring about this one cause does not inherently mean you don't care about other causes. In other words, you can care about more than one thing at once but you don't have to go around shouting from the rooftops that you care about breast cancer AND cervical cancer.

Oftentimes Black visibility inspires a DEFENSIVE reaction in non-Blacks (both white and POC) because Black visibility is seen as OFFENSIVE. Being proud of your Blackness is seen as offensive. Discussing Black issues is seen as offensive.

And people often end up making the assumption that you're being 'exclusive' when you talk about Black visibility as a reactionary, defensive move. whites and other nonblack POC have a habit of demanding that THEIR group be included in the discussion, or they co-opt Black movements into their movements and erase Black people entirely.

All of this stems from internalized racism and anti-Blackness. It has been ingrained within our society that Blackness is something bad, 'other,' and negative; triggering an extreme emotional response when non-Blacks are confronted with Black visibility. 'How dare you be Black and proud? How dare you want to speak publicly about Black issues?' If Black visibility triggers these types of feelings inside you, you should really step back and ask yourself why. Because just because you're a POC, doesn't mean you're not anti-Black.

PSA: Do Your Work

I'm sure you all are reeling from the results of the Department of Justice's recently released civil rights investigation on the Ferguson Police Department. The DOJ found 'a pattern of racial bias and targeted abuse of the Missouri city's minority population,' and reported that black residents of Ferguson were subjected to 93% of arrests and 85% of traffic stops between 2012 and 2014, despite making up just 67% of Ferguson's total population.

Other egregious offenses found included the fact that police dogs are often used on individuals when force is not necessary (fourteen people were bitten in the last few months alone- all Black), that Black people were "more than twice as likely as white drivers to be searched during vehicle stops, but 26% less likely to be found in possession of contraband," and the fact that revenue from fines issued during said traffic stops made up the bulk of the entire city's revenue. Mic.com went so far as to call the police department 'a kind of collection agency.'

Many white peoples reaction to this information has been to distance themselves from these facts, utilizing cognitive dissonance to create other reasons as to why the police department in Ferguson disproportionately targets Blacks and attempting to make it about ANYTHING but race. This has been a common practice for CENTURIES, wherein white people psychologically distance themselves from racism and oppression to preserve their own mental well being.

Lots of academic theories have been created around these concepts, including both 'white fragility (which is defined as 'a state in which even a minimum amount of racial stress becomes intolerable, triggering a range of defensive moves') and 'post traumatic slave syndrome' (which describes a set of behaviors, beliefs and actions associated with or, related to multi-generational trauma experienced by African Americans). white people use dissonance to retreat from race relations and to continue to enforce concepts of white supremacy and white fragility, attempting to make it Black people's responsibilities to use our energy to educate and inform them.

This brings me to a statement made by Toni Morrison during a lecture at Portland State University, where she says that, '"The very serious function of racism is distraction. It keeps you from doing your work. It keeps you explaining over and over again why you are here. Somebody says you don't have any language so you spend 20 years proving you do. Somebody says you don't have any culture so you dredge that up. None of that is necessary. There will always be one more thing. Complete your work without worry.' She also claims that racists NEED the energy that Black people expend trying to prove ourselves worthy; they thrive on it, and that instead of feeding racists, you should only put that energy into doing your work.

You are NEVER going to change the minds of people that are experiencing dissonance and are retreating into their bubble to protect their white fragility. They consume your energy with a voracious appetite, so do not give them what they desire above all things.

You have nothing to prove, and you know the truth: that you are free.

Reading List

1. "Investigation of the Ferguson Police Department." *United States Department of Justice.* United States Department of Justice Civil Rights Division, March 4, 2015. Web. <http://www.justice.gov/sites/default/files/opa/press-releases/attachments/2015/03/04/ferguson_police_departm ent_report.pdf/>.

2. Krieg, Gregory. "The DOJ Just Released Its Ferguson Investigation — And What They Found Is Horrifying." *Policy Mic.* Mic, March 4, 2015. Web. <http://mic.com/articles/111772/the-doj-just-released-its-ferguson-police-investigation-and-it-s-worse-than-you-thought?utm_source=policymicTBLR&utm_medium=mai n&utm_campaign=social/>.

3. Perez, Evan. "Justice report finds systematic discrimination against African-Americans in Ferguson." *CNN Politics.* CNN, March 4, 2014. Web. http://www.cnn.com/2015/03/03/politics/justice-report-ferguson-discrimination/>.

So, About That Patricia Arquette Oscar Speech... And Giuliana Rancic Thinks Zendaya Smells Like Weed? (On white Feminism and Stereotypes)

The Oscars just keep getting more and more racist, don't they?

Best Actress-winner Patricia Arquette has recently come under fire for a feminist, post-win Oscar speech that revolved around equal pay for women. While that sounds like a noble cause, her use of phrases like, "'To every woman who gave birth," "To every taxpayer and citizen of this nation," and, "We have fought for everybody else's equal rights," rubbed many the wrong way (What about women that haven't given birth? Non-taxpayers? Non-citizens?). Elaborating further backstage, Arquette also stated, "All the men that love women, and all the gay people, and all the people of color that we've all fought for... [need] to fight for us now.'"[23]

Yikes. Not only is this getting heavily into 'Oppression Olympics' territory, where members of marginalized groups pit themselves against each other over who is the 'most oppressed,'

---

[23] Marcotte, Amanda. "Patricia Arquette's Feminism: Only for White Women." *Slate.* Slate, February 23, 2015. Web. <http://www.slate.com/blogs/xx_factor/2015/02/23/patricia_arque tte_on_pay_equality_insulting_to_feminism.html/>.

her speech also buys into the idea of 'feminism' as something does that does not include men, or gay people, or people of color, etc.- in a nutshell, what many of us call, 'white feminism.'

This particular brand of feminism revolves around ignoring concepts of intersectionality, where, for example, race and sexuality affect gender. It's very easy for rich, cis, straight white women- like Patricia Arquette- to see feminism as this 'one thing,' because they benefit from privilege: he privilege of being rich, so poverty doesn't have to intersect with their feminism. The privilege of being cis, so being non-binary doesn't have to intersect with their feminism. The privilege of being straight, so sexuality doesn't have to intersect with their feminism. And the privilege of being white, so race doesn't have to intersect with their feminism.

In addition to Arquette's white feminist rant on Oscar night, fashion correspondent Giuliani Rancic also made headlines by claiming actress Zendaya Coleman's faux locs made her look like she smelled like 'weed' and 'patchouli oil' on the red carpet[24].

[24] Steiner, Amanda Michelle. "Zendaya Shames Giuliana Rancic for Oscar Night Comments About Her Dreadlocks." *People Magazine.* People, February 24, 2015. Web. <http://www.people.com/article/zendaya-blasts-giuliana-rancic-

Many pointed out that her comments had racist undertones, especially because Rancic recently praised white teen Kylie Jenner's similar hairstyle of fake dreads as 'hip' and 'edgy.' Zendaya blasted Rancic on Instagram, claiming she wore the hairstyle specifically because of the racial climate around natural hairstyles on Black people, and that she found Rancic's 'slurs' to be both offensive and stereotypical.

Rancic quickly said she never *meant* to be racist, and that she only meant to call Zendaya a 'hippie.' That's a nice backtrack, but especially when placed within the context of Rancic's glowing praise of Jenner's hair, it was clear that Rancic carries subconscious biases about Black hair. This is a classic case of 'Black features' being unacceptable on black bodies, but being accepted and praised on white bodies.

What next with these Oscars??? Sheesh.

oscars-dreadlocks-fashion-police/>.

Reading List

1. Steiner, Amanda Michelle. "Zendaya Shames Giuliana Rancic for Oscar Night Comments About Her Dreadlocks." *People Magazine.* People, February 24, 2015. Web. <http://www.people.com/article/zendaya-blasts-giuliana-rancic-oscars-dreadlocks-fashion-police/>.

2. Marcotte, Amanda. "Patricia Arquette's Feminism: Only for White Women." *Slate.* Slate, February 23, 2015. Web. <http://www.slate.com/blogs/xx_factor/2015/02/23/patricia_arquette_on_pay_equality_insulting_to_feminism.html/>.

3. Covert, Bryce, Petrohilos, Dylan. "The Gender Wage Gap Is A Chasm For Women Of Color." Think Progress, September 18, 2014. Web. <http://thinkprogress.org/economy/2014/09/18/3569328/gender-wage-gap-race/>.

4. Acosta, Grisely Y. "Racism begins in our imagination:" How the overwhelming whiteness of "Boyhood" feeds dangerous Hollywood myths." *Salon,* February 22, 2015. Web. <http://www.salon.com/2015/02/22/racism_begins_in_our_imagination_how_the_overwhelming_whiteness_of_boyhood_feeds_dangerous_hollywood_myths/>.

Reader Request: On 'Colorism'

Request from 'AcrossTheUniverse' on tumblr:

'Could you please make a video discussing how black girls are seen as less feminine than white girls. When people hear words like.......classical...elegant and so on. I know they don't think black. Like with Taylor swifts music video she only had white ballerinas and black girls twerking...I was like..."black girls do ballet Taylor." anyways I'm curious to hear your opinion and stuff because I don't know why this stereotype exist about black women..:/ Thanks!!!

Thanks for your request! Historically, colorism has revolved around the notion that darker skin is 'bad,' while lighter and white skin is 'good.' In American culture, this goes back to slavery, when lighter skin slaves were touted as 'superior,' and were allowed in the house, meanwhile darker skinned slaves were touted as 'inferior' and were forced to work out in the field; however, this is not only relevant for Black American people. It echoes across the world as a result of global colonization.

In practically every culture exists a caste system where the darker the skin, the lower a person's worth, and the lighter the skin (and closer to whiteness), the higher. We have internalized these concepts and continue to hand them down, making them still relevant and prevalent today.

Within the white gaze and Eurocentric standards of beauty, there is also this idea that whiteness/lightness is 'feminine' and Blackness/darkness is 'masculine,' leading to the attribution of dark skin as masculine on males and ugly on females, while lighter skin is seen as a feminine trait on males and a beautiful trait on females.

Many people attribute colorism to 'skin preference,' but I feel like skin preferences do not exist within a vacuum and the vast majority of them revolve around ingrained Eurocentric standards of beauty. Of course there are people who date whenever, regardless of preference. But when the vast majority of skin preferences revolve around terms like 'good hair' or 'pretty eyes' (or are fetishized around dark skin and masculinity), you have an issue that must be addressed.

Reading List

1. Dolan, Andy. "Why men prefer fair-skinned maidens and women like dark, handsome strangers." *The Daily Mail.* Daily Mail, March 17, 2008. Web. <http://www.dailymail.co.uk/sciencetech/article-535828/Why-men-prefer-fair-skinned-maidens-women-like-dark-handsome-strangers.html#ixzz3TR3z1PCy/>.

2. Hannon, Lance, DeFina, Robert. "When whites are guilty of colorism." *The Washington Post.* The Washington Post, November 7, 2014. Web. <http://www.washingtonpost.com/opinions/african-americans-still-face-colorism-based-on-their-skin-tone/2014/11/07/8a2ac124-607e-11e4-9f3a-7e28799e0549_story.html/>.

3. Jackson, Kristin Collins. "5 Truths About Colorism That I've Learned As a Black Woman In NYC." Bustle, November 18, 2014. Web. <http://www.bustle.com/articles/37427-5-truths-about-colorism-that-ive-learned-as-a-black-woman-in-nyc/>.

On 'White Male Rage'

Many have asked me why I felt the Chapel Hill shooting was a form of terrorism, and this really inspired to me FINALLY get my essay together on white male rage. Because IMO, it's very clear to say that what Craig Hicks did when he murdered Deah Shaddy Barakat, Yusor Mohammad Abu-Salha, and Razan Mohammad Abu-Salha[25] was a form of domestic terrorism.

Terrorism is simply defined as 'the use of violence and intimidation in the pursuit of political aims,' so one might wonder what was the 'political aim' of the Chapel Hill shooting. Well, I believe that all of white supremacy is a political cause; that white male entitlement is a political agenda and white power is a political agenda, just like black power or feminism are political agendas. So to kill someone in a fit of white male entitled rage for daring to challenge your white male authority, for daring to challenge the politics system of white supremacy just by EXISTING in what you feel is 'YOUR' white male space, is a

---

[25] Leszkiewicz, Anna. "The Chapel Hill shooting: White male atheist murders three Muslim students." *The New Statesman.* New Statesman, February 11, 2015. Web. <http://www.newstatesman.com/politics/2015/02/chapel-hill-shooting-white-male-atheist-murders-three-muslim-students/>.

political act of terrorism. That is a political response to a perceived threat to the political agenda that is white male supremacy, white power, and white privilege, and it is entirely fair IMO to call this terrorism and to call these people part of a domestic white terrorist group.

87% of mass U.S. shootings are committed by male Caucasians between the ages of 13 and 56, and the majority of these shootings revolve around perceived injustices from and revenge killings of people that fall outside of the entitled white male bloc (like women, like blacks, like Muslims, etc.). Elliott Rodgers revenge killed women because of the perceived injustice of them not dating him. The Columbine killer's revenge killed other students because they felt they were outcasts who were deprived of what was rightfully theirs in terms of popularity. There is a link between this sense of white male entitlement, this deservedness, and deadly rage.

White male entitled rage revolves around the entitlement that white men feel as a direct result of white male privilege, where they live in a world that is catered to them, revolves around them and where they are promised that they SHOULD have everything; and white male rage is the rage that they feel when that entitlement is not fulfilled. When it's blocked. When Muslims have the audacity to move in next door. When women have the audacity to not respond to dating advances. When Black people have the audacity to talk back, or attempt to vote, or not get on the sidewalk, or exercise their rights. When any of these things happen, their white male entitlement, their place as rightful masters of the universe, is challenged. And white men have been proven time and again to show that their response to this 'challenge,' is deadly rage, violence, and mass murder.

This whole shooting was about using violence to further a political cause, and that political cause was white supremacy. This was about using violence to further white entitlement, and it was about using violence to pacify Hicks' white male rage. This was about a white male atheist being so angry and so entitled that he feels his opinions on religion should be everyone's opinions, and he was willing to kill for that. That was a terrorist act.

But since Hicks is white, as with many other domestic terrorists, we will see him labeled instead as a 'lone wolf' or 'disturbed loner;' as 'mentally ill' or 'brilliant with problems,' as 'a good person who would NEVER do something like this.' All excuses made to continue to encourage this sense of white male entitlement.

White male rage is a thing. white domestic terrorism is a thing, and it is a direct result of the indoctrination our white supremacist society and white power as a political agenda. Being both white and male typically leads to an unchecked sense of white male privilege that can, and often does, become deadly when it turns into rage.

Reading List

1. Leszkiewicz, Anna. "The Chapel Hill shooting: White male atheist murders three Muslim students." *The New Statesman.* New Statesman, February 11, 2015. Web. <http://www.newstatesman.com/politics/2015/02/chapel-hill-shooting-white-male-atheist-murders-three-muslim-students/>.

2. Cooper, Britney. "White guy killer syndrome: Elliot Rodger's deadly, privileged rage." *Salon.* Salon, May 27, 2014. Web. <http://www.salon.com/2014/05/27/white_guy_killer_syndrome_elliot_rodgers_deadly_privileged_rage/>.

3. Hutchinson, Sikivu. "Nice White Boys Next Door and Mass Murder." *The Feminist Wire.* The Feminist Wire, December 16, 2012. Web. <http://thefeministwire.com/2012/12/nice-white-boys-next-door-and-mass-murder/>.

So, About That Jackie Robinson West Baseball Team Getting Stripped of Their National Title...

The all-Black Jackie Robinson West Little League team of Chicago, IL, was stripped of their National Title due to the fact that coaches and parents had falsified documents and maps to get around zoning requirements and recruit players. [26]

While it is EXTREMELY disappointing to discover these coaches and parents cheated, I was appalled to see the number of criticisms being leveled at the young Black players as being somehow complicit and fully aware of the scheme, along with thinly veiled racist references to Chicago 'gangsters and thugs' and expectations that the Black children COULDN'T have won against white Little League teams without cheating.

Statistics have proven that people see Black children as less innocent, more adult, and more cognizant of their actions than white children, and I am 100% convinced that had this team been all-white, there would have been much more sympathy for the players as *children* who were wronged by *adults,* instead

[26] Manchir, Michelle, Bowean, Lolly, Gross, Lexy. "Jackie Robinson West, city reel at loss of team's title." *The Chicago Tribune.* Chicago Tribune, February 11, 2015. Web. <http://www.chicagotribune.com/sports/chi-jackie-robinson-west-little-league-20150211-story.html#page=1/>.

of seeing them as somehow equally responsible and culpable for adult mistakes[27].

It is also extremely disheartening to see the number of people that expected Black children to naturally be cheaters or for white children to be inherently better than them at 'America's pastime.' [28]

I also find the lack of public interest in zoning and districting of inner-city neighborhoods to be telling. Many Black children use the addresses of family members and friends to get into better school districts or sports teams, and institutional discrimination in housing and racist zoning that trapped Black people in disadvantaged communities is one of the long-standing tenets of American racism.[29] Asking WHY the parents even felt

---

[27] "Black Boys Viewed as Older, Less Innocent Than Whites, Research Finds." *American Psychological Association.* APA, March 6, 2014. Web. <http://www.apa.org/news/press/releases/2014/03/black-boys-older.aspx/>.

[28] Bump, Philip. "People — Including Cops — See Black Kids as Less Innocent and Less Young Than White Kids." *The Wire.* The Wire, March 10, 2014. Web. <http://www.thewire.com/politics/2014/03/people-including-cops-view-black-kids-less-innocent-and-less-young-white-kids/359026/>.

[29] Hinkle, A. Barton. "Zoning's Racist Roots Still Bear Fruit."

compelled to falsify documents and recruit more kids could be an

interesting conversation to have.

Reason, April 2, 2014. Web.
<http://reason.com/archives/2014/04/02/zonings-racist-roots-still-
bear-fruit/>.

Reading List

1. Manchir, Michelle, Bowean, Lolly, Gross, Lexy. "Jackie Robinson West, city reel at loss of team's title." *The Chicago Tribune.* Chicago Tribune, February 11, 2015. Web. <http://www.chicagotribune.com/sports/chi-jackie-robinson-west-little-league-20150211-story.html#page=1/>.

2. Farrey, Tom, McDonald, Joe. "Little League punishes Chicago team." *ESPN Go.* ESPN, February 12, 2015. Web. <http://espn.go.com/chicago/story/_/id/12308988/little-league-strips-chicago-team-us-championship-suspends-coach/>.

3. Oz, Mike. "Jackie Robinson West should be stripped of title, says rival." *Yahoo! Sports.* Yahoo!, December 16, 2014. Web. <http://sports.yahoo.com/blogs/mlb-big-league-stew/rival-wants-jackie-robinson-west-stripped-little-league-championship-202447619.html/>.

4. "Black Boys Viewed as Older, Less Innocent Than Whites, Research Finds." *American Psychological Association.* APA, March 6, 2014. Web. <http://www.apa.org/news/press/releases/2014/03/black-boys-older.aspx/>.

5. Bump, Philip. "People — Including Cops — See Black Kids as Less Innocent and Less Young Than White Kids." *The Wire.* The Wire, March 10, 2014. Web. <http://www.thewire.com/politics/2014/03/people-including-cops-view-black-kids-less-innocent-and-less-young-white-kids/359026/>.

6. Hinkle, A. Barton. "Zoning's Racist Roots Still Bear Fruit." Reason, April 2, 2014. Web. <http://reason.com/archives/2014/04/02/zonings-racist-roots-still-bear-fruit/>.

7. Madrigal, Alexis C. "The Racist Housing Policy That Made Your Neighborhood." *The Atlantic.* The Atlantic, May 22, 2014. Web. <http://www.theatlantic.com/business/archive/2014/05/the-racist-housing-policy-that-made-your-neighborhood/371439/>.

So, About That Chapel Hill Shooting… On Domestic White Terrorism

I wrote this essay in the aftermath of the shooting death of three Muslims, Deah Barakat, 23, his wife, Yusor Mohammad Abu-Salha, 21, and her 19-year-old sister, Razan.[30] The reluctance of the media to call the bombing a 'terrorist attack' despite eyewitnesses seeing a white male leaving the device has clear racial implications. Well, here we are, barely a month later, and, again, we have an act of domestic white terrorism against people of color that is being compounded by media coverage that is late, sparse, and, above and beyond, going out of it's way to portray white suspects as anything but terrorists committing terrorist acts.

Terrorism is defined, quite simply, as 'the use of violence and intimidation in the pursuit of political aims,' and it is arguable that no other persons have been as forceful in using violence and intimidation against others as white people. From the mass

---

[30] Sullivan, Kevin, Berman, Mark, Kaplan, Sarah. "Three killed in shooting near University of North Carolina." *The Washington Post.* The Washington Post, February 11, 2015. Web. < http://www.washingtonpost.com/news/post-nation/wp/2015/02/11/three-killed-in-shooting-near-university-of-north-carolina/>.

genocide and diseases utilized against the indigenous Americans, to the bombs, lynchings[31], and water hoses of the American Civil Rights Movement to the police brutality and constant threat of armed vigilantes in the present day, white Americans have long exercised their right to intimidate and terrorize people of color with hardly any acknowledgment of or punishment for their deeds.

The media absolutely refuses to call the fear that white people enact onto others 'terrorism,' and, after dropping the ball on reporting this incident in the first place, they are now refusing to call the murders of three Muslim kids by a white man a hate crime. What will it take before we recognize that the systems of racism, white supremacy, and white entitlement/privilege in this country are deadly?

---

[31] The Editorial Board. "Lynching as Racial Terrorism." *The New York Times.* The New York Times, February 11, 2015. Web. <http://www.nytimes.com/2015/02/11/opinion/lynching-as-racial-terrorism.html/>.

Reading List

1. Sullivan, Kevin, Berman, Mark, Kaplan, Sarah. "Three killed in shooting near University of North Carolina." *The Washington Post.* The Washington Post, February 11, 2015. Web. < http://www.washingtonpost.com/news/post-nation/wp/2015/02/11/three-killed-in-shooting-near-university-of-north-carolina/>.

2. Goldberg, Michelle. "The Most Common Type of American Terrorist Is a White Man With a Weapon and a Grudge." The Nation, February 11, 2015. Web. <http://www.thenation.com/blog/197697/muslim-students-murdered-chapel-hill#/>.

3. The Editorial Board. "Lynching as Racial Terrorism." *The New York Times.* The New York Times, February 11, 2015. Web. <http://www.nytimes.com/2015/02/11/opinion/lynching-as-racial-terrorism.html/>.

On 'Black History Month'

I have a lot of conflicting feelings about Black History Month. On the one hand, I feel like something is better than nothing, but on the other hand, compartmentalizing ethnic/minority history further 'others' minorities and reinforces the idea that white/Eurocentric history is the standard for history in this country.

Without fail, every February you get the question: 'Why is there no white History Month?', and the answer is because every month is white History Month! We learn about white history every month of the year, with the implication that white history = American history just like white people = Americans. (And it's funny because for many Black Americans, American history is the ONLY history we have. Many of us can only trace our family lineage back a few generations until slavery. A lot of white families can trace their families back multiple generations to an 'Old Country,' yet are somehow seen as more American than ethnic minorities because they're white.)

Black people have been in this country for the last 500 years, but a common argument as to WHY we are not included in historical accounts of 'American' history is the assumption that we have been nothing but slaves or servants in this country. This couldn't be further from the truth. We have held important benchmarks in American History, from Fort Mose, the first sanctioned free Black city, established in 1738, to the artistic achievements of the Harlem Renaissance of the 1920s, to Jackie Robinson's success in Major League Baseball in 1947 and beyond.

Is this not 'American' history? And why must we learn a whitewashed, white supremacist version that seeks to portray American history as white and Black history as 'other' for 11 months out of the year?

P.S. One of the responses I've seen to this whitewashing of American history/'Othering' of minority history are attempts to normalize minority history through the use of hash tags like #HistoricPOC, which utilizes pictures of various POC throughout history engaging in American culture. While I feel like people's hearts are in the right place, POC is NOT synonymous with

Black, and celebrating non-Black POC during Black History Month is inappropriate and a form of Black erasure. Why #HistoricPOC and not #HistoricBlackPeople?

Talking about Black people *specifically* tends to make a lot of other, non-Black minorities/POC uncomfortable, and they often attempt to piggyback off of our movements by making them all-inclusive of POC. This has been discussed in my various 'All Lives Matter' videos and videos on anti-Blackness, because, in my opinion, anti-Blackness is at the root of a lot of it.

Sometimes people and their individual struggles need to be addressed specifically, and sometimes it can be erasure and offensive to lump all minorities together under the umbrella term of 'POC.'

So, About That 'Fantastic Four' Reboot... Why Isn't Sue Storm Black?

Ugh. I am SO NOT HERE for this 'Fantastic Four' reboot.[32]

While the casting of Michael B. Jordan as Johnny Storm/The Human Torch sounds progressive on paper, it is disheartening to see Kate Mara cast as his sister, Sue Storm/The Invisible Woman. The backstory as to why the brother and sister are two different races has yet to be revealed (some have theorized an interracial marriage between Johnny and Sue's parents and others have posited that one of them was possibly adopted), but it most certainly would have been easier to just cast the entire Storm family as Black, and one has to wonder why they didn't do that?

As Chris Rock pointed out while doing his 'Top Five' promo tour a few months ago[33], while Hollywood is still sorely

---

[32] Blay, Zeba. "The 'Fantastic Four' Reboot Casting: Progressive Or Not?" Shadow and Act. Indiewire Blogs, February 20, 2014. Web. <http://blogs.indiewire.com/shadowandact/the-fantastic-four-reboot-casting-progressive-or-not/>.

[33] Rock, Chris. "Chris Rock Pens Blistering Essay on Hollywood's Race Problem: "It's a White Industry."" *The Hollywood Reporter*. The Hollywood Reporter, December 3,

lacking in diversity, Black actors are still seen as more viable in film. Meanwhile Black actresses are practically invisible, and a moviegoer and go months without seeing a Black woman in a speaking or main role. As generally happens when racism and sexism intersect, we also often see a complete and utter disregard for Black women in the generally white, Male-driven superhero films: white women are typically utilized to fulfill the 'sex/gender' quota, meanwhile Black men are hired to fit the 'race' quota. There is no space for Black women (not named 'Storm').

Without even getting into the conversation of why there are still race and sex/gender quotas in Hollywood, it is distinctly telling that Kate Mara was cast to play Sue Storm and not a Black actress. It feels very deliberate, and gives the sense of taking one step forward, and two steps back. Instead of REALLY taking the plunge and casting a full Storm family of Black actors, they tokenize Michael B. Jordan and continue the idea that Black female superheroes don't exist or somehow aren't as viable as their male counterparts. And that freaking SUCKS.

2014. Web. <http://www.hollywoodreporter.com/news/top-five-filmmaker-chris-rock-753223#sthash.4DtOTBQY.dpuf/>.

Reading List

1. Blay, Zeba. "The 'Fantastic Four' Reboot Casting: Progressive Or Not?" *Shadow and Act.* Indiewire Blogs, February 20, 2014. Web. <http://blogs.indiewire.com/shadowandact/the-fantastic-four-reboot-casting-progressive-or-not/>.

2. Rock, Chris. "Chris Rock Pens Blistering Essay on Hollywood's Race Problem: "It's a White Industry."" *The Hollywood Reporter.* The Hollywood Reporter, December 3, 2014. Web. <http://www.hollywoodreporter.com/news/top-five-filmmaker-chris-rock-753223#sthash.4DtOTBQY.dpuf/>.

So, About That Anthony Mackie Interview...

RESPECTABILITY POLITICS ARE STUPID.

I find myself saying this after reading a particularly offensive interview given by Black actor Anthony Mackie[34], where, among other things, he stated that he sat his nephew down to watch 'The First 48' after the boy expressed a desire to grow dreadlocks. Mackie then went on to say, "...everybody you see on that show, that's doing something wrong, they're Black dudes with dreadlocks. So, do you want to be seen as part of the problem or do you want to be an individual?"

This is a disgusting display of respectability politics and victim blaming, all of which revolve around the idea that, 'If you hadn't done x, then y wouldn't have happened.' If you didn't wear a short skirt, then you wouldn't have been raped. And if you weren't wearing a hoodie (or if you didn't have dreadlocks, according to Anthony Mackie) you wouldn't have been racially profiled. This leaves absolutely no accountability for racist, sexist

---

[34] Witherspoon, Chris. "Anthony Mackie on Selma's Oscar snub: 'People are just tired of being bombarded with race right now." The Grio, January 20, 2015. Web. <http://thegrio.com/2015/01/20/anthony-mackie-selma-oscar-snub-black-white/>.

systems that are in place and puts the full burden of responsibility onto the VICTIM. Instead of examining what led up to the rape or the racial profile, we just chalk it up to individual incidents.

I once saw a really great Janet Mock/bell hooks panel[35] where Mock says that people do this as a defense mechanism because then they can feel 'safe.' If we're talking about individuals that did something wrong and 'brought this on themselves,' then we can feel safe because WE would never do that. But if we're talking about oppressive systems that are in place then it can happen to ANYONE. And that's a scary feeling, I know, but we have to face reality.

A lot of people have also identified with what Mackie was saying as a part of 'survival skills' and a way to 'camouflage' themselves in white society. But how far do we allow that to go? One day it's wearing hoodies, one day it's wearing natural hair, one day it's driving a nice car, etc. These are all deflections from the real issue, which is being BLACK in America. And, again, instead of examining the systems and stereotypes that make white

---

[35] The New School. "bell hooks - Are You Still a Slave? Liberating the Black Female Body | Eugene Lang College." Online video clip. YouTube. YouTube, May 7, 2014. Web. https://www.youtube.com/watch?v=rJk0hNROvzs/>.

people afraid when they see a Black person with deadlocks or that makes them suspicious when they see a Black person with nice things, you're putting the onus on the victim to 'camouflage' themselves to fit in and make white people comfortable. The idea is still that white people are the 'bosses' and we are not equals. We have to fit into some 'white standard' to be seen as human. And that's a problem.

Reading List

1. Witherspoon, Chris. "Anthony Mackie on Selma's Oscar snub: 'People are just tired of being bombarded with race right now." *The Grio.* The Grio, January 20, 2015. Web. <http://thegrio.com/2015/01/20/anthony-mackie-selma-oscar-snub-black-white/>.

2. The New School. "bell hooks - Are You Still a Slave? Liberating the Black Female Body | Eugene Lang College." Online video clip. *YouTube.* YouTube, May 7, 2014. Web. https://www.youtube.com/watch?v=rJk0hNROvzs/>.

The Problem of Race and Gender in Hollywood

This essay is going to be about the extremely whitewashed nominations for the 2015 Academy Awards, where, for the first time since 1998, no actors of color were nominated in any of the major categories[36]. Women in technical fields like direction, cinematography, and editing were also snubbed, being left off of all of the nominations outside of the Best Actress and Best Supporting Actress categories.

These two issues of race and gender poignantly intersected in the shocking snubbing of Ava DuVernay, director of the Best Picture-nominated film, 'Selma.' DuVernay, who was widely expected to be nominated for the well-reviewed drama, would have made history as the first Black woman ever to be nominated for a Best Director Academy Award.

There are typically two main arguments used to defend the clear bias towards white men in Hollywood: the first centers around the belief that art is being judged strictly off of merit without regards to race or gender, and that the white men 'just

[36] Siede, Caroline. "Selma's snubs speak volumes about Hollywood and the Oscars." *The A.V. Club*. A.V. Club, January 15, 2015. Web. <http://www.avclub.com/article/selmas-snubs-speak-volumes-about-hollywood-and-osc-213889/>.

happen' to be rewarded every time. The second claims minorities and women 'just aren't interested' in working in film, and therefore white men dominate because there simply is no competition. Both concepts could not be further from the truth.

I'm sure we can all agree that films SHOULD be based off their merits and not the race (or gender) of their creators. But they're not. Because if you truly believe that's what happening, then you truly believe that white men consistently make better movies, are better actors, directors, writers, editors, cinematographers, and producers than women or minorities. When an ENTIRE year's worth of nominations is majority white and male, either the Academy has a problem with race and gender OR white men are just better at making movies. And I think we can all agree that white men aren't just naturally better at making movies than minorities and women, can we not? The Academy only THINKS white men are the only ones that make movies worth awarding every year.

There also is no shortage of qualified Black or female creatives- just look to the current diversity in television as proof of that. Black people (and women) grow up watching and loving movies just like everyone else- aka white men- and they similarly wish to create movies and be a part of Hollywood. It's not that they just 'don't want to go into these professions;' it's that they are not given the same opportunities because of racism and sexism.

Oscar voters are 93% white and 76% male, and they often only reward movies that center around a very specific white male experience. But when the Academy only recognizes white male-dominated films year after year, they continuously send the message that these are the only films worth creating, watching, financing, and distributing. And while the Oscars are not the end-all and be-all of good art (clearly), there is a also certain amount of prestige and attention that comes with a nomination, and being recognized in front of your peers.

What a Hollywood really interested in diversity would do is reward great work by all filmmakers, regardless of gender or race, and encourage people from all walks of life to create by representing them in film and television.

Reading List

1. Siede, Caroline. "Selma's snubs speak volumes about Hollywood and the Oscars." *The A.V. Club.* A.V. Club, January 15, 2015. Web. <http://www.avclub.com/article/selmas-snubs-speak-volumes-about-hollywood-and-osc-213889/>.

2. Murphy, Shaunna. "Yes, The Oscars Are So White, And Here's Why That Matters." *MTV News.* MTV, January 15, 2015. Web. <http://www.mtv.com/news/2050617/2015-oscar-nominations-selma-snubbed/>.

On Racism, Sexism, Azealia Banks, and Misogynoir

This essay is going to focus on misogynoir and the undercurrents of racism and sexism that I personally feel surround the criticism of rapper Azealia Banks. After another highly publicized Twitter beef that involved rappers Lupe Fiasco and Kid Cudi[37], I came to the conclusion that the outspoken female emcee is often referred to using sexist and racist language that attacks her personally rather than discussing her views and opinions.

I find it interesting that after the heated exchange between Cudi, Lupe, and Banks, everyone is focusing on Lupe and Azealia but no one is really talking about Kid Cudi's involvement[38]. Cudder said the same thing as Banks regarding Kendrick Lamar's statements (that Kendrick shouldn't speak for the entire race, that

---

[37] Peters, Mitchell. "Kid Cudi & Lupe Fiasco Argue on Twitter Over Kendrick Lamar's Michael Brown Comments." *Billboard*. Billboard, January 11, 2015. Web. <http://www.billboard.com/articles/columns/the-juice/6436483/kid-cudi-lupe-fiasco-argue-on-twitter-over-kendrick-lamar-billboard-cover-interview/>.

[38] Guardian Music. "Azealia Banks and Kid Cudi lay into Kendrick Lamar over Ferguson." *The Guardian*. The Guardian, January 12, 2015. Web. <http://www.theguardian.com/music/2015/jan/12/azealia-banks-kid-cudi-lay-into-kendrick-lamar-ferguson/>.

what Kendrick said was wrong, etc.) and he also got into a VERY ugly and personal war of words with Lupe on Twitter. For some reason, though, people are really glossing over this and, instead, are sticking it to Azealia. Is it sexist that we pile on Azealia for being a 'loudmouth ghetto chick' but we completely ignore Black males that say and do the exact same things as her?

Banks has been targeted for being 'rude,' 'classless,' 'crazy,' 'loudmouth,' 'ghetto,' 'bitchy,' or 'messy,' but known internet trolls like Lupe Fiasco, 50 Cent, or Chris Brown are rarely referred to using the same gendered and/or racially-motivated language. While Lupe, a troll that sits on Twitter and gets messy with EVERYONE, was the one that actually started the confrontation with both Banks and Kid Cudi, no one seems to talk about the fact that he was the instigator or use the same phrases they use when they refer to Banks.

IMO, the criticism of Banks has a decidedly racist and sexist undercurrent, especially when terms like 'emotional,' 'bitter,' and 'jealous' are used. These are phrases you hardly ever see leveraged at males (well, males not named Drake or Kanye) or at non-Black women. Many of her detractors can't even explain what they disagree with or don't like about her without using racist and sexist language. Hate her or love her, agree or disagree, the undercurrent of misogynoir in the criticism of Banks rubs me the wrong way.

I'm not saying EVERY person that comes at Banks is sexist or racist. But I do think there is an undercurrent of racism and sexism to the fact that we care so much about Black female trolls but don't give a fuck about rude, obnoxious male trolls. 50 Cent is a rude and mean troll, but his rants don't make it to the front page every week. And again, even when we do talk about it he is hardly ever referred to as 'ghetto,' 'loudmouth,' 'classless,' etc. Those are words we typically use when we talk about a Black woman. It's interesting to me.

Reading List

1. Peters, Mitchell. "Kid Cudi & Lupe Fiasco Argue on Twitter Over Kendrick Lamar's Michael Brown Comments." *Billboard.* Billboard, January 11, 2015. Web. <http://www.billboard.com/articles/columns/the-juice/6436483/kid-cudi-lupe-fiasco-argue-on-twitter-over-kendrick-lamar-billboard-cover-interview/>.

2. Guardian Music. "Azealia Banks and Kid Cudi lay into Kendrick Lamar over Ferguson." *The Guardian.* The Guardian, January 12, 2015. Web. <http://www.theguardian.com/music/2015/jan/12/azealia-banks-kid-cudi-lay-into-kendrick-lamar-ferguson/>.

So, About That Rapper, Logic, and White Passing Privilege

This is an essay about white privilege and the rapper Logic, who has been garnering a lot of mainstream attention recently since he released a debut album after years of releasing mixtapes underground. As another white rapper being pushed by the white mainstream music industry, he is a shining example of the whitewashing of hip-hop as well as of all-encompassing white privilege. Many of his fans, however, feel that the fact that he is of mixed race (but white passing) means he therefore does not receive white privilege.

I decided to write this essay because of what seemed like a general misunderstanding of how white privilege and white passing privilege works. white privilege is based off of skin color and appearances, so actual parentage or genetic makeup does not play a role. If you appear white, even if you aren't technically 'white,' you will still benefit from white privilege. When buyers, consumers, record label executives, etc., look at an album cover or a picture of Logic, they see a white face and make a snap judgment, and as a biracial artist who appears more 'white,' he has a 'safe' (aka white) look and will be marketed to mainstream (aka white) audiences easier than biracial artists that appear more 'Black,' like J. Cole or Drake.

Black/Brown skin & bodies are seen as inherently dangerous and savage, while white bodies are seen as the norm, 'safe,' and universal. So despite being biracial, Logic's white skin has allowed him white passing privilege and the opportunity to blow up (especially if he begins to make 'pop rap' like 'Fancy' or 'Thrift Shop') due to his appearance as a 'white rapper.'

I'm not saying Logic hasn't worked hard, or that he isn't talented. But I AM saying that at this point in his career, if he wanted to, he could sit back and let the mainstream take him the rest of the way simply because he has white skin, biracial or not.

And that, my friends, is white (passing) privilege.

Reading List

1. Associated Press. "Mom Blames Race For Fatal Police Shooting Of Son Darrien Hunt." *Black Voices.* The Huffington Post, September 14, 2014. Web. <http://www.huffingtonpost.com/2014/09/14/darrien-hunt_n_5817940.html/>.

2. Palazzolo, Joe. "Wide Racial Divide in Sentencing." *The Wall Street Journal.* WSJ, February 14, 2013. Web. <http://www.wsj.com/articles/SB10001424127887324432004578304463789858002/>.

So, About That Antonio Martin Shooting... and The Power of Suggestion

This essay focuses on my thoughts about the recent shooting of Antonio Martin, the Black teen was killed in Berkley, MO (only miles away from Ferguson) on Christmas Eve, 2014[39]. There has been a swirl of controversy around this case for numerous reasons, including the fact that the St. Louis Police Department has released grainy, blurry surveillance camera footage claiming Martin was carrying a gun, as well as the fact that the officer who shot Martin had both a body camera and dash cam in his car but neither was turned on.

I'm concerned about the release of the surveillance footage because, although it is of extremely poor quality, you have individuals ready to believe that they *see* a gun just because it has been suggested to them by the police. How can you 'clearly' see a gun when the video itself isn't clear? If it hadn't already been suggested to you that you see a gun, might you see something

---

[39] Martellaro, Alexandra. "Second night of protests after Antonio Martin shooting." *USA Today.* USA Today, December 25, 2014. Web. <http://www.usatoday.com/story/news/nation/2014/12/25/protesters-berkeley-shooting/20889139/>.

else? A wallet? A cell phone? (It has been speculated that Martin was in fact holding up a cell phone, not a weapon.)

There have been multiple studies that show that not only do we have an unconscious bias against Black and Brown bodies as being inherently dangerous, we also have a tendency to misidentify them as being armed and/or aggressive even when they are not. In a recent study done by Keith Payne, an assistant professor of psychology at Ohio State University, he found that '...people are more likely to misidentify tools as guns when they are first linked to African Americans, at least under extreme time pressure.'

Payne and his colleagues conducted experiments in which subjects viewed a picture of a man, quickly followed by a picture of either a tool or a gun. When asked to identify whether the second picture was a tool or a gun, participants were much more likely to misidentify a tool as a gun when the preceding picture was that of an African American. They were also more likely to misidentify a gun as a tool when the preceding picture was that of a white man. So it isn't far-fetched to wonder if perhaps the 'gun' was in fact, a cell phone.

But even if Martin DID have a gun, that still did not give police the right to execute him. Cops neutralize armed suspects without using lethal force EVERY DAY, and it is the job of a police officer to apprehend and arrest, not to play judge, jury, and executioner. James Eagan Holmes and Dzhokhar Tsarnaev are just two of the names of armed suspects in public places that were successfully apprehended by police without the use of deadly force. Google 'armed suspects apprehended by police' and you can come up with a hundred more instances where police have used non-lethal methods to neutralize and arrest armed (and unarmed) suspects.

THEY DON'T HAVE TO KILL YOU. Police make a CHOICE to shoot to kill, and more often than not, they are choosing to use deadly force on Black and Brown bodies.

Reading List

1. Martellaro, Alexandra. "Second night of protests after Antonio Martin shooting." *USA Today*. USA Today, December 25, 2014. Web. <http://www.usatoday.com/story/news/nation/2014/12/25/protesters-berkeley-shooting/20889139/>.

2. Vibes, John. "Could Antonio Martin Have Pointed A CAMERA At The Officer Who Shot Him?? The Free Thought Project, December 27, 2014. Web. <http://thefreethoughtproject.com/antonio-martin-pointed-camera-officer-shot-him/#TwO4TpKg4xiRIqfi.99/>.

3. Payne, Keith. "WHITES MORE LIKELY TO MISIDENTIFY TOOLS AS GUNS WHEN LINKED TO BLACK FACES." *Research News*. Research News, n.d. Web. <http://researchnews.osu.edu/archive/gunbias.htm/>.

4. Payne, Keith. "Weapon Bias; Split-Second Decisions and Unintended Stereotyping." *Sage Journals*. A Journal of the Association for Psychological Science, n.d. Web. <http://cdp.sagepub.com/content/15/6/287.short/>.

5. Levin, Diane. "A video game tests racial bias – and the willingness to pull the trigger." Mediation Channel, April 6, 2008. Web. <http://mediationchannel.com/2008/04/06/a-video-game-tests-racial-bias-and-the-willingness-to-pull-the-trigger/>.

So, About Those 2015 Grammy Nominations...

This is an essay about the sorry state of the Grammy Awards and the slow whitewashing of mainstream music. After last year's sweep of the rap categories by duo Macklemore and Ryan Lewis (for the now ironically-named rap album, 'The Heist') over Kendrick Lamar's critically-acclaimed, 'good kid, m.a.a.d city,' a lot of music listeners have been questioning the validity of the Grammy Awards and the prescience of the committee voters. It appears white artists are being heavily awarded and touted for their work, while Black artists are either left off entirely or pigeon-holed into the recently-created 'Urban Contemporary Album' genre.

It's extremely troubling that a racialized code word like 'urban' has made it into the high-profile awards ceremony, and many also wonder about the music industry's creation of sub-genres like 'neo-soul' and the habit of pushing Black artists into said sub-genres and out of mainstream categories like pop and r&b[40]. Singer Beyoncé is a prime example of this push: her

---

[40] Cliff, Aimee. "10 Reasons The Grammys Are As White As You Think They Are." *The Fader.* The Fader, December 13, 2014. Web. <http://www.thefader.com/2014/12/12/10-reasons-the-grammys-are-as-white-as-you-think-they-are/>.

critically acclaimed fifth album, 'Beyoncé,' while being nominated for Album of the Year, Best R&B song, and Best R&B performance, was not nominated for R&B Album of the Year, Record of the Year, or Song of the Year. Instead she finds herself relegated to the 'Best Urban Contemporary Album' category.

Newcomers YG (rapper), DJ Mustard (producer), and fka twigs (singer), also all saw themselves left out although they each released some of the most critically-acclaimed work in 2014; every Record of the Year, Song of the Year, and Best New Artist nominee is white. Pop-rapper Iggy Azalea has been the first rapper to ever be cross-nominated in different genres, and other heavily Black-influenced white artists see themselves at the top of the 'Big Four' categories.

Many fear that this is removing opportunities for Black artists to gain mainstream interest and recognition. There have also been concerns that the Grammy committee is too old, too white, and too mainstream to properly assess the quality of music in little-known or culturally significant genres like rap or r&b, and instead just gives the awards away to well-known (and typically white) names for publicity and viewership.

Reading List

1. Cliff, Aimee. "10 Reasons The Grammys Are As White As You Think They Are." *The Fader.* The Fader, December 13, 2014. Web. <http://www.thefader.com/2014/12/12/10-reasons-the-grammys-are-as-white-as-you-think-they-are/>.

2. DeVille, Chris. "Making Sense Of The 2015 Grammy Nominations." *Stereogum.* Stereogum, December 5, 2014. Web. <http://www.stereogum.com/1723204/making-sense-of-the-2015-grammy-nominations/franchises/essay/>.

3. Kenner, Rob. "Hate Me Now: What It's Like To Be A Grammy Voter." *Complex UK.* Complex, January 20, 2014. Web. <http://uk.complex.com/music/2014/01/how-does-grammy-voting-work/>.

So, About Those Sony Email Leaks... We Live In A Society of 'Racism Without Racists'

This is going to be a quick essay about the Great Sony EmailGate of 2014, which involves leaked personal emails exchanged between Sony Pictures executives[41]. Sony co-chair Amy Pascal and Oscar-winning producer Scott Rudin are some of the most recent execs to get emails hacked, in some of which they express racist commentary about comedian Kevin Hart, who they called a 'greedy whore,' and also about POTUS Barack Obama, whom they posit 'must like Kevin Hart movies' and 'probably loved Django [along with other 'Black' movies like '12 Years A Slave'].'

The emails were blasted by the media as 'racially insensitive,' and the two have since publicly apologized. What I (and many others, like award winning content creator, writer, and producer Shonda Rhimes[42]) find to be problematic about this

---

[41] McCalmont, Lucy. "Sony execs apologize for racist Obama emails." Politico. Politico, December 11, 2014. Web. <http://www.politico.com/story/2014/12/sony-executives-apologize-for-racist-barack-obama-emails-113508.html/>.

[42] Dockterman, Eliana. "Shonda Rhimes Slams 'Racist' Leaked Sony Emails." Time. Time, December 11, 2014. Web.

entire thing is the lack of willingness to call these acts 'racist' outright, and the expectation that an apology and claim of 'I'm not racist!' is enough to mollify the public.

These two high-level Hollywood execs and their casual racism are perfect examples of white moderates in our current society of 'racism without racists.' The term, coined by sociologist Eduardo Bonilla-Silva, theorizes 'that we have gotten past our history of overt racism and [instead] have become a country that is built on "racism without racists."' He goes on to state that, "The 'new racism' is subtle... and institutionalized." So while Pascal and Rudin might not consider themselves 'racists,' per se, they are still holding onto unconscious biases about Black culture and behavior, and as people in high positions, this has a subtle trickle down effect of possibly influencing the actors they hire, the movies they finance, etc. (All of which has also been recently thrown into the spotlight thanks to a series of searing essays on race in Hollywood by comedian Chris Rock[43].)

<http://time.com/3631127/shonda-rhimes-sony-emails/>.
[43] Rock, Chris. "Chris Rock Pens Blistering Essay on Hollywood's Race Problem: "It's a White Industry."" The Hollywood Reporter. The Hollywood Reporter, December 3, 2014. Web. <http://www.hollywoodreporter.com/news/top-five-filmmaker-chris-rock-753223/>.

Pascal and Rudin are not alone in their subtle-yet-evident racist perception of Black Americans. Many white people fall into the 'white moderate' category of not considering themselves to be racist although they hold onto unconscious biases and racist beliefs, keeping the national conversation on race completely stagnant.

Reading List

1. McCalmont, Lucy. "Sony execs apologize for racist Obama emails." *Politico*. Politico, December 11, 2014. Web. <http://www.politico.com/story/2014/12/sony-executives-apologize-for-racist-barack-obama-emails-113508.html/>.

2. Dockterman, Eliana. "Shonda Rhimes Slams 'Racist' Leaked Sony Emails." *Time*. Time, December 11, 2014. Web. <http://time.com/3631127/shonda-rhimes-sony-emails/>.

3. Blake, John. "The new threat: 'Racism without racists.'" *CNN*. CNN, November 27, 2014. Web. <http://www.cnn.com/2014/11/26/us/ferguson-racism-or-racial-bias/>.

4. Rock, Chris. "Chris Rock Pens Blistering Essay on Hollywood's Race Problem: "It's a White Industry."" *The Hollywood Reporter*. The Hollywood Reporter, December 3, 2014. Web. <http://www.hollywoodreporter.com/news/top-five-filmmaker-chris-rock-753223/>.

On Tamir Rice, Akai Gurley, and a Culture of Fear

This essay will be on the heartbreaking stories of both Tamir Rice[44] and Akai Gurley[45], so here it is. This is a hard story for me to write about, because the lack of compassion and empathy being shown for these stolen lives, especially in the death of 12-year-old Rice, is astounding.

Rice was a child, at most a 7th grader, and yet police have called him 'a guy,' a 'young male,' and 'maybe 20.' Many *regular* (aka non-police) Americans have also wondered, 'Why did he have the toy gun?' and stated, 'His age doesn't give him an excuse to make bad choices'/'He should be old enough to know better.' This inability to see Black youth as innocents capable of making mistakes corresponds with studies that have shown average white citizens see Black children as more mature at a younger age and believe Black people feel less pain. It also places

---

[44] Balko, Radley. "But for video: Tamir Rice edition." The Washington Post. The Washington Post, December 2, 2014. Web. <http://www.washingtonpost.com/news/the-watch/wp/2014/12/02/but-for-video-tamir-rice-edition/>.

[45] Associated Press. "Akai Gurley, Unarmed Man, Shot By NYPD." HuffPost Crime. The Huffington Post, November 22, 2014. Web. <http://www.huffingtonpost.com/2014/11/22/akai-gurley-nypd_n_6205492.html/>.

the entire onus for Rice's death on his small shoulders for his so-called 'mistakes.'

Where is the blame for the manufactures that mass-produce and market realistic-looking toy guns to children? Where is the blame for the culture that glorifies violence and gun use? (And I'm not talking about the much vilified 'Black Thug Culture,' either; we are heading into the holiday season where the American classic 'A Christmas Story' will be played non-stop on television: a movie about a child who receives a realistic-looking BB gun for Christmas. Where are the letters of outrage?) Where is the blame for the superhero movies and comic books marketed towards children where the primary protagonists use guns and other violent weapons? Rice's desire to play with a toy gun did not spontaneously appear out of a vacuum, and his playing with it in a public place does not constitute a 'mistake.'

All people make mistakes. This does not give police the right to shoot first and ask questions later, as they have been implying with statements like, 'We had NO CHOICE but to shoot him!' What about the many mass shootings where perpetrators have been apprehended and arrested without the use of deadly force? Police somehow find plenty of ways not to use lethal force with white suspects, and, in acknowledgement of this, a quote has been going around stating that 'Privileged kids go to counseling, and poor kids go to jail.' I have to add that, 'Black kids go to the grave,' because the same reasoning's used every day to justify mass shootings (like mental illness or problems at home) and to recommend counseling are now being utilized to smear, demonize, and justify why a 12-year-old child was taken out before he had the opportunity to become a threat.

At the end of the day, this is not about individual cops being bad people. This is not about isolated racial incidents. This is not about a realistic-looking toy. This is about a culture of fear surrounding 'superhuman' Black people and the ensuing demonization of Black victims and communities as an unstoppable threat. This fear in and of itself is racist and until this anti-blackness that is ingrained within our society is recognized, there can be no progress.

Reading List

1. Balko, Radley. "But for video: Tamir Rice edition." *The Washington Post.* The Washington Post, December 2, 2014. Web. <http://www.washingtonpost.com/news/the-watch/wp/2014/12/02/but-for-video-tamir-rice-edition/>.

2. Associated Press. "Akai Gurley, Unarmed Man, Shot By NYPD." *HuffPost Crime.* The Huffington Post, November 22, 2014. Web. <http://www.huffingtonpost.com/2014/11/22/akai-gurley-nypd_n_6205492.html/>.

3. Silverstein, Jason. "I Don't Feel Your Pain: A failure of empathy perpetuates racial disparities." *Slate.* Slate, June 27, 2013. Web. <http://www.slate.com/articles/health_and_science/science/2013/06/racial_empathy_gap_people_don_t_perceive_pain_in_other_races.html/>.

So, About That St. Louis Rams Protest...

During a Sunday Night Football game in late 2014, one that pitted the St. Louis Rams against the Oakland Raiders, five Black Rams players (Tavon Austin, Kenny Brit, Stedman Bailey, Jared Cook, and Chris Givens) chose to come out onto the field with their hands in the signature 'Hands up, Don't Shoot' pose made famous during protests in Ferguson, MO[46]. The team won the game 52-0, but that blowout was nothing compared to the blowback the team received for the player's silent pre-game protest. The St. Louis Police Officers Association immediately released an official statement calling for the players to be fined and suspended, and many fans blasted the team on social media Sunday night, claiming politics in the game is 'inappropriate.'[47]

---

[46] Strauss, Chris. "Rams players come out with hands up in pre game intros." For The Win. USA Today, November 30, 2014. Web. http://ftw.usatoday.com/2014/11/rams-hands-up-pregame/>.

[47] Bernhard, Jimmy. "SLPOA condemns Rams display." KSDK. KSDK, December 7, 2014. Web. <http://www.ksdk.com/story/news/local/2014/11/30/stl-police-officers-association-condemns-rams-display/19721979/?hootPostID=56e4d621f410c5ee1ef0c0b0696f34f8/>.

I can't help but wonder, when did complicit silence about race from public figures become acceptable? Previously in history, Black actors, musicians, and athletes were public symbols of the Civil Rights Movement and activism, and while we look back on these moments as 'iconic,'[48] our current society blasts modern-day public figures as 'inflammatory' when they voice their opinions on race and race relations in this country. In a time where *normal* people are able to be as vocally opinionated as ever through social media, we have entered into a strange vacuum where, conversely, public figures are expected to keep quiet about potentially polarizing topics.

Are we living in a Gestapo-run police state? It is absurd that any time public figures speak out against race and/or the police force there is an immediate and virulent backlash.

---

[48] "1968: Black athletes make silent protest." BBC News. BBC, October 17, 2014. Web. <http://news.bbc.co.uk/onthisday/hi/dates/stories/october/17/newsid_3535000/3535348.stm/>.

Reading List

1. Strauss, Chris. "Rams players come out with hands up in pre game intros." *For The Win.* USA Today, November 30, 2014. Web. <http://ftw.usatoday.com/2014/11/rams-hands-up-pregame/>.

2. Bernhard, Jimmy. "SLPOA condemns Rams display." *KSDK.* KSDK, December 7, 2014. Web. <http://www.ksdk.com/story/news/local/2014/11/30/stl-police-officers-association-condemns-rams-display/19721979/?hootPostID=56e4d621f410c5ee1ef0c0b0696f34f8/>.

3. "1968: Black athletes make silent protest." *BBC News.* BBC, October 17, 2014. Web. <http://news.bbc.co.uk/onthisday/hi/dates/stories/october/17/newsid_3535000/3535348.stm/>.

Thoughts on Ferguson: America and the Legacy of Violence

When the grand jury released their decision on the Mike Brown case- no indictment- I was rocked by emotion. I was angry, sad, disappointed… but I was not surprised.

A portion of protestors rioted at the decision, although by and large, demonstrations have been peaceful[49]. I personally have no issues with violent rebellion, as citizens are protesting an unjust government and justice system and I feel they can do that however they see fit. But there has been a lot of pushback against the violent tactics, which I find to be both hypocritical and nonsensical, especially because we are a nation built on violence.

Almost every major American event in history has been catalyzed by violence. Violence literally built this country: from the American genocide against Native Americans, to the Revolutionary War, to the holocaust of slavery (which built the American Economy), to the bloody Civil War to free the slaves. The government also utilizes violence to deal with American issues like the 'War' on Terror and the 'War' on Drugs.

---

[49] Bennett, Dashiell, Berman, Russell. "No Indictment." The Atlantic. The Atlantic, November 25, 2014. Web. <http://www.theatlantic.com/national/archive/2014/11/ferguson-verdict-grand-jury/383130/>.

People are creating a rhetorical world where violence is never the answer, but they don't want to apply that on a systemic level. If violence is never the answer, then why do we even have military units? Armed forces? Navy? Army? Why do cops carry guns? If we literally should be pacifist and nonviolent then all of these agencies must be stripped of weapons and dismantled.

American culture is also mired in violence: people claim to be nonviolent but love the Avengers, Batman, Spider-Man, and The Hunger Games: all fictional characters that fight for justice through violence. People riot over sports events and pumpkins. So what about black and brown bodies rioting for justice makes you uncomfortable to the point where you want to retreat from violence and create entire fantasy worlds where 'violence is never an option?'

Think about it.

Reading List

1. Bennett, Dashiell, Berman, Russell. "No Indictment." *The Atlantic*. The Atlantic, November 25, 2014. Web. <http://www.theatlantic.com/national/archive/2014/11/ferguson-verdict-grand-jury/383130/>.

2. McClam, Erin. "Ferguson Cop Darren Wilson Not Indicted in Shooting of Michael Brown." *NBC News*. NBC, November 25, 2015. Web. <http://www.nbcnews.com/storyline/michael-brown-shooting/ferguson-cop-darren-wilson-not-indicted-shooting-michael-brown-n255391/>.

3. Reilly, Ryan J. "Ferguson Officer Darren Wilson Not Indicted In Michael Brown Shooting." *HuffPost Politics*. The Huffington Post, November 24, 2014. Web. < http://www.huffingtonpost.com/2014/11/24/michael-brown-grand-jury_n_6159070.html/>.

4. Basu, Moni, Yan, Holly, Ford, Dana. "Fires, chaos erupt in Ferguson after grand jury doesn't indict in Michael Brown case." *CNN News*. CNN, November 25, 2014. Web. < http://www.cnn.com/2014/11/24/justice/ferguson-grand-jury/>.

So, About That TIME Banned Words Poll...

This is a short essay about a rather ridiculous *TIME Magazine* 2014 poll, titled, 'Which Word Should Be Banned in 2015?'[50] While it included only two tech/business terms ('influencer' and 'disrupt'), many people have pointed out the racist, sexist nature of the vast majority of the list, which mainly targeted African-American Vernacular English slang words like 'bae' and 'turnt' along with words mostly popularized and utilized by young females, like 'I can't even,' 'sorry not sorry,' and 'obvi.' *TIME* has also been criticized for including the word 'feminist' on the list.

The author tried to give an explanation on her Twitter account, where she claimed the word 'feminist' was included based off of trends in the media, and not due to any hatred of the women's rights movement. Yet I can't help but wonder, why is the popularity of the word 'feminist' a bad thing? People want to talk about feminism, yay! As long as there is inequality between the sexes (which there is) we should continue to talk about it and

---

[50] Steinmetz, Katy. "Which Word Should Be Banned in 2015?" TIME Magazine. TIME, November 12, 2014. Web. <http://time.com/3576870/worst-words-poll-2014/>.

work towards changing things. Not to mention that if trendiness is all that's necessary to get on the list, why wasn't a word like, 'Ebola,' which surely has had more mentions this year than 'feminism,' included?

I also want to add that *TIME*'s previous hit lists have generally included many words appropriated from Black people into mainstream culture (like 'YOLO,' 'twerk,' and 'swag') and this is a clear indicator of the vicious and parasitic nature of appropriation, wherein white people Columbus something from Black culture, run it into the ground, then claim it's 'dead' and 'vote it off the island.' The lists also typically include phrases reaped from youth culture (and especially youth internet culture), like 'OMG' and other internet-cetric abbreviations.

The fact that prominent words in Black, youth, or female culture are seen as 'annoying' or 'overly trendy' and in need of being banned year after year (this is TIME's fourth year creating the list) is extremely problematic and indicative of the rampant racism, sexism, and ageism/classism/elitism in our society. Just because Black people, young people, and women use a word doesn't mean it's stupid or ridiculous.

TIME Magazine can literally suck it, obvi. Sorry not sorry.

Reading List

1. Steinmetz, Katy. "Which Word Should Be Banned in 2015?" *TIME Magazine.* TIME, November 12, 2014. Web. <http://time.com/3576870/worst-words-poll-2014/>.

2. Allen, Samantha. "Feminist, Bae, Turnt: Time's 'Worst Words' List Is Sexist and Racist." *The Daily Beast.* The Daily Beast, November 13, 2014. Web. <http://www.thedailybeast.com/articles/2014/11/13/feminist-bae-turnt-time-s-worst-words-list-is-sexist-and-racist.html?utm_source=feedburner&utm_medium=feed&utm_campaign=Feed:+thedailybeast/articles+(The+Daily+Beast+-+Latest+Articles)/>.

3. Polo, Susana. "'Time Magazine Asks "Is Feminist the Worst Word of 2014?" in New Poll. We Have an Answer For Them." *The Mary Sue.* The Mary Sue, November 12, 2014. Web. <http://www.themarysue.com/time-magazine-feminist/>.

4. Moss, Rachel. "Time Magazine Suggests 'Feminist' Should Be A Banned Word In 2015 - The World Is Not Happy About It." *HuffPost Women.* The Huffington Post, November 13, 2014. Web. <http://www.huffingtonpost.co.uk/2014/11/13/times-magaizine-feminist-ban-reaction_n_6150358.html/>.

So, About That Nicki Minaj 'Only' Lyric Video...

I kind of liked it?

I know this essay is going to get a lot of you up in arms, but hear me out. When I initially viewed the lyric video for Nicki Minaj's newest single, 'Only,' I thought it was a great use of an allegory. Allegories are defined as 'literary or rhetorical devices that convey hidden meanings through symbolic figures, actions, imagery, and/or events;' and use of allegories 'create the moral, spiritual, or political meaning the author wishes to convey.'

As an allegory, Nicki's video makes perfect sense. She utilizes Nazi Germany imagery in order to convey the idea of her label Young Money as a fascist regime, where she is the dictator and the feature artists on the song (Lil Wayne, Drake, and Chris Brown, respectively) are her cabinet.[51] She also pointedly did NOT include any images of Jewish peoples, or any type of victims, for that matter; the imagery solely focuses on the 'Young Money Army' and their leader.

---

[51] Johnson, Jr., Billy. "Nicki Minaj Slammed for Anti-Semitic Images in Lyric Video." Yahoo! Music. Yahoo!, November 10, 2014. <https://music.yahoo.com/blogs/music-news/nicki-minaj-slammed-for-anti-semitic-images-in-lyric-video-174111139.html/>.

Of course she picked Nazis, one of the most easily recognizable regimes, to express these concepts of authority and dictatorship: allegories by nature are meant to 'readily illustrate complex ideas and concepts in ways that are comprehensible to its viewers, readers, or listeners.' She could have picked a less recognizable (and less controversial) regime, but would the video have been as effective if she had utilized Fidel Castro and the Communist Party of Cuba? Kim Jong-Un and the Democratic People's Republic of Korea? Joseph Stalin and the Communist Soviet Union? Probably not.

Nazism, the Holocaust, and Jews have been prominent figures in pop culture for years and are widely used to emphasize points about dictatorships, terrorism, seclusion, victimization, and fear, among other concepts. Is this use inherently anti-Semitic? If the art stands up to critical review, I'm inclined to say no.

I also have to add that I find it extremely interesting that people find the use of Nazi imagery and leaders to be offensive, but do not find the use of mobsters and gang leaders/gang violence to be offensive (like rappers naming themselves after a mobster that has had extremely destructive effects on a Black community, for example), or the use of famous political figures known for mass deaths or defamation to be offensive.

P.S. With that being said, I am glad she apologized for offending people and mentioned reference points for the video, but I don't like her throwing in that, 'Jews created it,' the equivalent of, 'I can't be racist, I have Black friends.'

No Bueno.

Reading List

1. Johnson, Jr., Billy. "Nicki Minaj Slammed for Anti-Semitic Images in Lyric Video." *Yahoo! Music.* Yahoo!, November 10, 2014. <https://music.yahoo.com/blogs/music-news/nicki-minaj-slammed-for-anti-semitic-images-in-lyric-video-174111139.html/>.

A Quick Word On Lena Dunham and White Feminism

This short essay is about the shit-storm that is Lena Dunham. There have been plenty of pieces made about how sick and disturbing the published excerpts from her memoirs are, so while I briefly touched on that, I also wanted to talk about the way race ties into the defense of Dunham. white feminism inherently ties to white privilege and ideals about white supremacy, and white feminists will ruthlessly defend Lena Dunham despite her many sexist and racist transgressions because she has the 'complexion for protection.'

Artists of color are never afforded the same opportunities; chance after chance to explain themselves and continue to be praised and create, and it's even larger than just art: on a grand scale, people of color are not allowed innocence or the room to fail and make mistakes. Failure is a luxury of white privilege, as is the ability to chalk it up to *life experiences* and move on. Failures and flaws are instead utilized as fodder against people of color to demonize and vilify us, justify our incarcerations, social statuses, problems, and even deaths.

Reading List

1. Awesomely Luvvie. "About Lena Dunham's Memoir, Overshare and Lack of Boundaries." Awesomely Luvvie, November 2, 2014. Web. <http://www.awesomelyluvvie.com/2014/11/lena-dunham-memoir.html/>.

2. Shapiro, Ben. "Lena Dunham Threatens To Sue Truth Revolt For Quoting Her." *Truth Revolt.* Truth Revolt, November 3, 2014. Web. <http://www.truthrevolt.org/commentary/lena-dunham-threatens-sue-truth-revolt-quoting-her/>.

#BrandBlackface

This essay revolves around a topic I've wanted to discuss for a while; which is that of influence versus power. Many people seem to think the two are synonymous, but I disagree, especially when it comes to the influence of the Black community on mainstream culture vs. the power it actually wields within said culture.

This will be framed around a conversation I had on instagram about a slang-y tweet sent out by the IHOP Twitter account: 'Pancakes on fleek.' This is the latest incident in a recent series where white-owned corporations appropriate slang, AAVE, and other cultural colloquialisms in order to monetize Black culture without actually experiencing or contributing to the Black American experience.

Many people feel that this is an important step in advertising because of the visibility it creates for Black culture. I disagree, however, and feel like the Black people that created these terms are not getting paid or recognized in any tangible way for their influence, making this purely a reaping of Black youth culture for profit. IMO, if corporations like IHOP really wanted to increase visibility or cultural understanding between Black Americans and mainstream corporate culture, they would put their money where their mouths are and hire Black interns, Black sales reps, Black social media managers, etc. Instead, white people are placed in these positions and serve as conduits into Black culture. It is inauthentic and falls in line with the history of white people in this country appropriating *subversive* Black culture for a 'cool' factor and profit.

Not only does this dehumanize our culture into something *other* and exotic (and only worth value because of what can be co-opted, monetized, and consumed), but it also keeps Black creators in a permanent low-caste position of influence without real power.

Reading List

1. Sloane, Garett. "Are Brands on Fleek With Slangy Tweets? IHOP Explains Its Hip New Voice 'Back that stack up." *AdWeek*. AdWeek, October 23, 2014. Web. <http://www.adweek.com/news/technology/whos-behind-these-crazy-ihop-tweets-160955#.VFjWSYo8KnP/>.

So, It's Only Street Harassment If He's Black? Oh, Ok.

Woo boy. This essay is a response to the fervor that's surrounding a certain catcalling video, one that went viral on YouTube, amassing millions of hits. When I first saw it, I was immediately concerned with the fact that a white woman is shown as a monolithic representation of *all women*, as well as the fact that the only people that harass her were men of color (typically Black and Hispanic/Latino)[52].

I felt that the entire video was furthering a narrative where the innocent white woman is threatened by the inherently violent and aggressive man of color, and it was revealed today that the company (which itself is named after appropriating and stereotyping AAVE) edited out any heckling perpetrated by white men in the video. This fosters a false sense of security among women that white men are *safe* (as opposed to men of color who are dangerous) and undermines the message of how dangerous and pervasive catcalling actually is. ANY man can

---

[52] Rosin, Hanna. "The Problem With That Catcalling Video." Slate. Slate, October 29, 2014. Web. <http://www.slate.com/blogs/xx_factor/2014/10/29/catcalling_video_hollaback_s_look_at_street_harassment_in_nyc_edited_out.html?wpsrc=fol_fb/>.

perpetrate street harassment- not just men of color. And white men don't get to sit back in their chairs in complacency as they watch videos like this and pat themselves on the back for not 'being like that.'

white feminists have a habit of attempting to separate race from sex and gender, and many are defending the message of the video while giving a pass to the racist undertones. This is EXTREMELY problematic and undermines the nature of feminism as being something for all women.

Reading List

1. Rosin, Hanna. "The Problem With That Catcalling Video." *Slate.* Slate, October 29, 2014. Web. <http://www.slate.com/blogs/xx_factor/2014/10/29/catcalling_video_hollaback_s_look_at_street_harassment_in_nyc_edited_out.html?wpsrc=fol_fb/>.

Leave Iggy Azalea Alone! Just Leave Her Alone! (On Black Men and White Women)

Before I start, I want to make it known that I am not against IR relationships, I do think two people of a different race can fall in love and be happy. I am specifically not talking about people of a different race that are in healthy, loving, respectful relationships. I am specifically talking about degrading and hurtful relationships between BM/WW that carry echoes of slavery. If this is not you, please do not be offended. If this you, well, hit dogs holler.

Although her career seemed to burnout as quickly as it started, it is easy to remember mainstream media headlines blaring with headlines highlighting a 'rap beef' between rapper Snoop Dogg and Iggy Azalea. The media almost took on the tone of a lynch mob, claiming Snoop 'viciously attacked' Iggy, and her manager, T.I., eventually stepped in to insist on an apology.

This incident falls in context with the thinking of the past 400 years that indicates that Black men and white women have a peculiar and symbiotic relationship, wherein each gets something:

1. white women treat Black men as an animalistic protector, like a pet dog that protects them and also offers them a

walk on the 'wild side' sexually. Throughout history, Black men have been seen as 'mandingos,' and known for sexual prowess, hypersexuality, and hypermasculinity[53]. white women also often cite 'protection' as a main reason for their attraction, but what about this Black man makes you feel protected that you don't get from your own kind? Does he remind you of an animal? A dog? A bear?

    2. Black men, in turn, treat white women as something pure, fragile, innocent, and worthy of protection. Colorism also plays a part in this, as lighter and whiter skin colors are often equated to hyperfemininity, innocence, and superiority. Black men that suffer from a colonized mind also wish to have what their colonizer has: they wish to eat his food, sit at his table, sleep in his bed, and fuck his daughter. white women are the ultimate status symbol. Why does this white woman make you want to protect her and not your own kind? Does she seem innocent? Pure? Fragile? Madonna-like? This all falls under the 'white gaze'

---

[53] 1. Khan, Aaminah. "The Semiotics of Race, or: Walks on the Wild Side." Black Girl Dangerous, April 28, 2014. Web. <http://www.blackgirldangerous.org/2014/04/semiotics-race-walks-wild-side/>.

that paints Eurocentric beauty as an ultimate as opposed to black women who are painted as 'strong,' 'independent,' and 'masculine.'

Note: Black women, in contrast, are not seen as pure or innocent, but self sufficient, strong, and independent. This is a holdover from slavery (where Black women were worked just as hard a Black men) and also the habit of matriarchy in the black community, where Black women are seen as strong creatures that can do it all and 'don't need no man.' The white gaze also has a habit of masculinizing dark skin so Black women are seen as more masculine, and not feminine/fragile or worthy of protecting, especially dark skinned Black women.

Reading List

1. Khan, Aaminah. "The Semiotics of Race, or: Walks on the Wild Side." Black Girl Dangerous, April 28, 2014. Web. <http://www.blackgirldangerous.org/2014/04/semiotics-race-walks-wild-side/>.

2. Djvlad. "Lord Jamar: Iggy Azalea's Poppin Because She's White." Online video clip. *YouTube.* YouTube, Jul 13, 2014. Web. <https://www.youtube.com/watch?v=iyql_BxdCSY&app=desktop/>.

The Disposable Life and 'Suspicious' Death of Vonderrit Myers

On of the eve of the National March on Ferguson and the #FergusonOctober movement, another Black youth has lost his life at the hands of police. 18-year-old Vonderrit Myers was gunned down by an off-duty St. Louis Police Officer who followed him after deeming Myers and his friends 'suspicious' figures on a street corner.[54] The as-yet unnamed cop felt Myers 'acted aggressively' and 'held his pants in a manner that suggested he had a weapon.' Although the details are still unclear, at the end of the day, Myers was not arrested; instead, he was killed by a cop who did not attempt to apprehend him and instead played judge, jury, and executioner when he had no proof Myers actually did anything wrong.

The off-duty officer admitted to making a U-turn to go at the boys while seeing no crime being committed, proceeded to chase them although he saw no crime being committed, then fired

---

[54] Barbash, Fred, Phillip, Abby. "Fatal shooting of 18-year-old by off-duty police officer ignites protests in St. Louis." The Washington Post. The Washington Post, October 9, 2014. Web. <http://www.washingtonpost.com/news/morning-mix/wp/2014/10/09/crowds-in-streets-of-st-louis-after-fatal-shooting-by-off-duty-police-officer/>.

upon and killed Vonderrit Myers, who was committing no crime. He pursued and attacked them for literally no reason.

white people have committed mass murders, terrorist acts, serial killings, etc.- only to be treated with the utmost care to ensure they are apprehended, brought in alive, and able to receive their due process from a judge or jury of their peers. This is one of the inherent privileges of being white. Black lives, in contrast, are treated as disposable, especially once it has been decided we are acting 'suspiciously' or 'aggressively.' There is no need to determine innocence or guilt, no respect for Black life, and no justice served.

Reading List

1. Barbash, Fred, Phillip, Abby. "Fatal shooting of 18-year-old by off-duty police officer ignites protests in St. Louis." *The Washington Post.* The Washington Post, October 9, 2014. Web. <http://www.washingtonpost.com/news/morning-mix/wp/2014/10/09/crowds-in-streets-of-st-louis-after-fatal-shooting-by-off-duty-police-officer/>.

2. Hartmann, Margaret. "Police Officer Fatally Shoots Teenager, Sparking Protests in St. Louis." *The New York Magazine.* New York Mag, October 9, 2014. Web. <http://nymag.com/daily/intelligencer/2014/10/st-louis-police-officer-fatally-shoots-teenager.html?mid=twitter_dailyintelligencer/>.

Racism Is Not Voldemort and Paul Callan Is Ridiculous

The interwebs have been ablaze with a video of a Black family being terrorized by police officers in Hammond, Indiana[55]. When Lisa Mahone was pulled over for not wearing a seatbelt, she complied with police requests for her license and registration. However, when they asked her boyfriend, Jamal Jones, for his identification, things go south.

Jones doesn't have identification and the police immediately draw a weapon when he goes to get papers out of his backpack that show who he is. There are two children in the back, aged 14 and 7, who are recording the altercation, which ended with police breaking the passenger side window, tasering Jones, and dragging him out of the car to arrest him.

Discussing the incident on a CNN panel, legal analysts Sunny Hostin, a Black woman, and Paul Callan, a white man, got into a screaming match over whether or not this issue is about race. Callan claimed there was no 'evidence' to indicate that this

---

[55] Ford, Quinn. "Hammond police sued over use of Taser during traffic stop." The Chicago Tribune. Chicago Tribune, October 7, 2014. Web. <http://www.chicagotribune.com/news/local/breaking/chi-hammond-police-taser-story.html/>.

was racially motivated, while Hostin said that her life as a woman of color in this country is evidence enough.

This is a common practice in the United States, where white people have a habit of requiring 'evidence' before they will believe something is about race, and instead insist people of color are 'making this about race' when it is not. What constitutes 'evidence?' How do you compare your experiences as a person with inherent privilege to the experiences of people that have to cope with life every day as a second-class citizen?

This type of thinking undermines positive race-relations and puts the onus of 'proving' racism 'actually exists' on the victims of racism, which is a Herculean task. Either you accept that racism DOES, in fact, exist, and move forward actively working to combat it, or you are a part of the problem.

Reading List

1. Wemple, Erik. "CNN panel erupts in argument about cops and racial profiling." *The Washington Post.* The Washington Post, October 7, 2014. Web. <http://www.washingtonpost.com/blogs/erik-wemple/wp/2014/10/07/cnn-panel-erupts-in-argument-about-cops-and-racial-profiling/>.

2. Ford, Quinn. "Hammond police sued over use of Taser during traffic stop." *The Chicago Tribune.* Chicago Tribune, October 7, 2014. Web. <http://www.chicagotribune.com/news/local/breaking/chi-hammond-police-taser-story.html/>.

Raven-Symone Isn't Gay Or Black; Also, Don't Label Me A Human, I Am A Meat Popsicle

I'm sure you guys have heard of Raven-Symone's controversial interview with Oprah, during which she proclaimed she 'doesn't like labels' and refused to label herself as gay or African-American, while simultaneously labeling herself a human, American, and colorless[56]. Head-scratcher, right? Her use of labels like 'American' and 'colorless' show she doesn't actually dislike all labels, but SPECIFIC ones, like 'Black' and 'homosexual.'

Many people are latching onto her proclamations of being colorless and 'not African-American' because they seem like a slap in the face to Black audiences that have watched her playing a Black girl on predominantly Black shows over the years. But I also found her reluctance to be labeled 'gay' disconcerting because it reeked of internalized homophobia.

---

[56] McRady, Rachel. "Raven-Symone: I Don't Want to Be Labeled as Gay or African American." US Weekly. US Magazine, October 6, 2014. Web. <http://www.usmagazine.com/celebrity-news/news/raven-symone-dont-want-labeled-gay-african-american-2014610#ixzz3FTAQXl2K/>.

Statements like these, while they sound nice on the surface, are indicative of larger issues our society has as a whole with 'labels.' Labels are not inherently a bad thing; only when framed within the context of a society built on white supremacy, hegemony, sexism, racism, and heteronormativity do labels like 'African-American' and 'gay' (and 'woman' and 'bisexual' and so many more) become bad things.

Labeling yourself 'colorless' certainly won't shield yourself or others from racism, nor will it make it magically go away. Labeling yourself 'a human who loves humans' also will not shield you from homophobia or hate crimes against gay people, nor will it make homophobia magically go away.

People willing to stand up publicly as members of marginalized groups and say that they DEMAND equality are the only ways to bring about equality in this society. The beauty of America is NOT in being colorless or label-less, but in embracing our colors and differences and treating each other as equals. Not pretending we are all the same.

Reading List

1. McRady, Rachel. "Raven-Symone: I Don't Want to Be Labeled as Gay or African American." *US Weekly.* US Magazine, October 6, 2014. Web. <http://www.usmagazine.com/celebrity-news/news/raven-symone-dont-want-labeled-gay-african-american-2014610#ixzz3FTAQXl2K/>.

2. Howerton, Jason. "Just Watch Oprah's Reaction After Actress Rejects Labels and Declares Herself Not 'African-American." *The Blaze.* The Blaze, October 6, 2014. Web. <http://www.theblaze.com/stories/2014/10/06/just-watch-oprahs-reaction-after-actress-rejects-labels-and-declares-herself-not-african-american/>.

3. D'Addario, Daniel. "Raven-Symoné's No-Labels Approach to Sexuality Isn't Anything New." *TIME Magazine.* TIME, October 6, 2014. Web. <http://time.com/3474880/raven-symone-that-s-so-raven-oprah-winfrey/>.

'Thug Kitchen (Thug Racists)' and Coded Language

This is an essay about 'Thug Kitchen' (or 'Thug Racists,' as they will now and forevermore be known) and their food blog[57]. A lot of people seem to be confused (or, at the very least, feigning confusion) about what specifically makes the blog problematic, so I wanted to write this short piece that went into detail about racism and coded language.

The Thug Racists are utilizing colloquialisms, vernacular, and speech patterns associated with Black people (AAVE slang, Ebonics, etc.) along with coded language like 'thug' and 'gangsta'-terms that are commonly associated with Blackness. In addition to keeping their true identities as white people a secret, they essentially ran a blog comprised of literary blackface, where they mocked stereotypical Black culture (thugs, gangsters, swearing, phrasing) and contrasted it against luxury recipes and photographs.

This is a common practice in America, where, to 'stand out and be different,' white people utilize Black mannerisms to be

---

[57] Dickson, Akeya. "Thug Kitchen: A Recipe in Blackface." The Root. The Root, September 30, 214. Web. <http://www.theroot.com/articles/culture/2014/09/thug_kitchen_a_recipe_in_blackface.html/>.

edgy, cool, and funny. This is like the food version of Miley Cyrus. They also exacerbated the mockery in their commercial for the Thug Racism cookbook, which doesn't utilize a single person of color and instead clearly makes a play off of Black slang words versus upstanding white citizens.

The whole thing is highly offensive, especially at a time when Black people are being murdered and criminalized for being 'thugs,' 'gangsters,' and 'suspicious.' It is pure racism and it sickens me.

Reading List

1. Dickson, Akeya. "Thug Kitchen: A Recipe in Blackface." *The Root.* The Root, September 30, 214. Web. <http://www.theroot.com/articles/culture/2014/09/thug_kit chen_a_recipe_in_blackface.html/>.

2. Desmond-Harris, Jenee. "8 Sneaky Racial Code Words and Why Politicians Love Them." *The Root.* The Root, March 15, 2014. Web. <http://www.theroot.com/articles/politics/2014/03/_racial _code_words_8_term_politicians_love.html/>.

3. Carlos, Jordan. "Do You Speak Gentrification?" *The Huffington Post.* The Huffington Post, September 30, 2014. Web. < http://www.huffingtonpost.com/jordan-carlos/new-york-gentrification_b_5902732.html/>.

4. Saul, Isaac. "What Richard Sherman Taught Us About America." *HuffPost Sports.* The Huffington Post, January 20, 2014. Web. <http://www.huffingtonpost.com/isaac-saul/what-richard-sherman-taught-us_b_4631980.html/>.

The New York Times, 'Angry Black Women,' and Accountability

I wrote this essay after catching wind of a New York Times piece written by their chief television critic, Alessandra Stanley[58]. With the incendiary term 'Angry Black Woman' in the title, Stanley's piece centered around the upcoming show 'How To Get Away With Murder,' starring Viola Davis and produced by successful television writer Shonda Rhimes, and referenced numerous offensive stereotypes with regards to Black women (including the aforementioned 'Angry Black Woman' trope)[59].

When the backlash hit, Stanley responded defensively, stating the 'Twittersphere' did not properly assess her piece (stating it was not offensive once you got past 'the first 140 characters') and that she was known for using inflammatory

---

[58] Sullivan, Margaret. "An Article on Shonda Rhimes Rightly Causes a Furor." The Opinion Pages. The New York Times, September 22, 2014. Web. <http://publiceditor.blogs.nytimes.com/2014/09/22/an-article-on-shonda-rhimes-rightly-causes-a-furor/?_php=true&_type=blogs&_php=true&_type=blogs&partner=rss&emc=rss&smid=tw-nytimes&_r=1&/>.

[59] Etkin, Jaimie. "Shonda Rhimes Fires Back At The Critic Who Called Her An "Angry Black Woman." Buzzfeed. Buzzfeed, September 19, 2014. Web. <http://www.buzzfeed.com/jaimieetkin/shonda-rhimes-response-to-angry-black-woman#261jgz9/>.

statements in her work. She did not apologize and merely stated it was never her 'intent' to make anyone feel bad. In a more detailed explanation from a chief Times editor, they express regret that the piece made it past three editors and detail the lack of diversity and 'blind spot' at the newspaper.

Merely saying you did not 'purposely' intend to be racist is not enough. There is no sense of accountability for racist behavior in our society, intentional or not; instead, there is an attitude of placing a higher value on the intent than the action. There is no understanding of the concept that racist actions are racist and need to be addressed, regardless of intent.

Reading List

1. Sullivan, Margaret. "An Article on Shonda Rhimes Rightly Causes a Furor." *The Opinion Pages.* The New York Times, September 22, 2014. Web. <http://publiceditor.blogs.nytimes.com/2014/09/22/an-article-on-shonda-rhimes-rightly-causes-a-furor/?_php=true&_type=blogs&_php=true&_type=blogs&partner=rss&emc=rss&smid=tw-nytimes&_r=1&/>.

2. Etkin, Jaimie. "Shonda Rhimes Fires Back At The Critic Who Called Her An "Angry Black Woman." *Buzzfeed.* Buzzfeed, September 19, 2014. Web. <http://www.buzzfeed.com/jaimieetkin/shonda-rhimes-response-to-angry-black-woman#261jgz9/>.

3. Prince, Richard. "NY Times TV Critic Defends 'Angry Black Woman' Story.'" *The Root.* The Root, September 21, 2014. Web. <http://www.theroot.com/blogs/journalisms/2014/09/new_york_times_tv_critic_alessandra_stanley_defends_angry_black_woman_story.html?wpisrc=newstories/>.

4. Paskin, Willa. "Shonda Rhimes Is Not an "Angry Black Woman," New York Times." *Slate.* Slate, September 19, 2014. Web. <http://www.slate.com/blogs/browbeat/2014/09/19/shonda_rhimes_an_angry_black_woman_wrong_new_york_times_she_is_so_much_more.html/>.

5. Littleton, Cynthia. "New York Times Critic Blames Twitter for Shonda Rhimes Story Backlash." *Variety Magazine.* Variety, September 19, 2014. Web. <http://variety.com/2014/tv/news/shonda-rhimes-new-york-times-1201309560/>.

39758540R00114

Made in the USA
San Bernardino, CA
03 October 2016